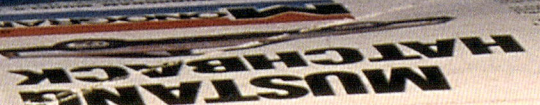

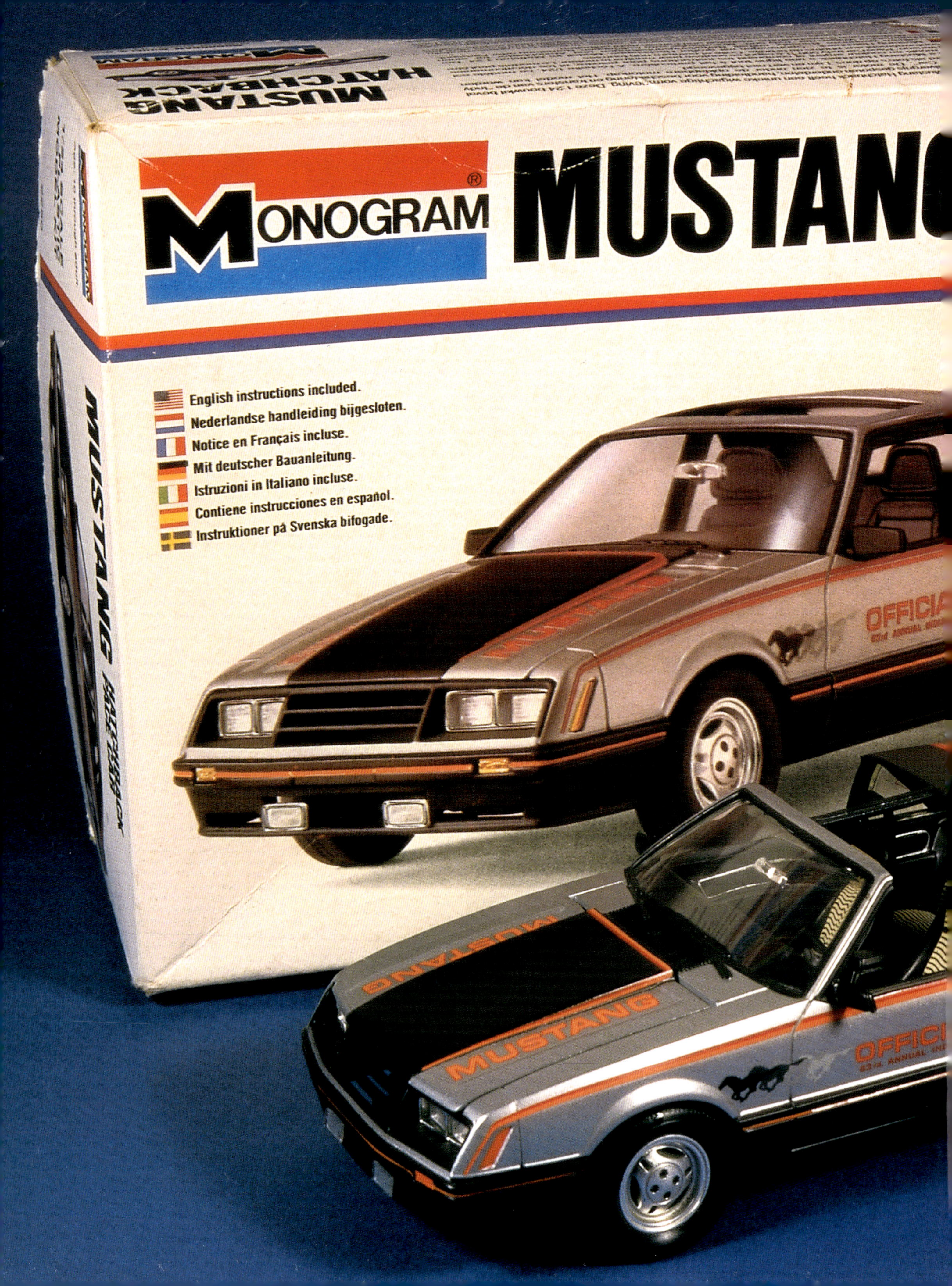
MONOGRAM
MUSTANG
English instructions included.
Nederlandse handleiding bijgesloten.
Notice en Français incluse.
Mit deutscher Bauanleitung.
Istruzioni in Italiano incluse.
Contiene instrucciones en español.
Instruktioner på Svenska bifogade.
MUSTANG
HATCHBACK
MUSTANG

Mustang
Collectibles

Bill Coulter

MBI Publishing Company

First published in 2002 by MBI Publishing Company, 380 Jackson Street, Suite 200, St. Paul, MN 55101-3885 USA

© Bill Coulter, 2002

All rights reserved. With the exception of quoting brief passages for the purposes of review, no part of this publication may be reproduced without prior written permission from the Publisher.

The information in this book is true and complete to the best of our knowledge. All recommendations are made without any guarantee on the part of the author or Publisher, who also disclaim any liability incurred in connection with the use of this data or specific details.

We recognize that some words, model names and designations, for example, mentioned herein are the property of the trademark holder. We use them for identification purposes only. This is not an official publication.

MBI Publishing Company books are also available at discounts in bulk quantity for industrial or sales-promotional use. For details write to Special Sales Manager at Motorbooks International Wholesalers & Distributors, 380 Jackson Street, Suite 200, St. Paul, MN 55101-3885 USA

Library of Congress Cataloging-in-Publication Data Available

ISBN 0-7603-1173-0

On the front cover: A wide variety of some of the great Mustang collectibles.

On the frontispiece: This Ertl 1/18th scale diecast 1968 Mustang comes from the American Muscle series. This limited-production Taska Ford version is of a popular and victorious vintage Super Stock drag car that was driven by Hubert Platt.

On the title page: Monogram struck a chord with modelers and racing fans with this version of the 1979 Mustang Indy pace car. In the background is an unbuilt Monogram kit No. 2250. I built the finished model shown here.

On the back cover: Mustang collectibles remain plentiful. Here is a trio of interesting items. The Department 56 Christmas specialty line includes this Uptown Motors Ford billboard as part of their recent Original Snow Village Series, that also featured a 1965 Mustang GT convertible. This metal tin box with a hinged lid features a 1965 convertible, and is manufactured by the Tin Box Company. The Enesco music box on the right has a 1/43rd scale 1965 Mustang that revolves as Del Shannon's "Little Runaway" plays.

Edited by Amy Glaser
Designed by Dan Perry

Printed in Hong Kong

Contents

	Acknowledgments	6
	Introduction	7
Chapter 1	Concepts and Show Cars	13
Chapter 2	Generation I, 1964 1/2–1966	19
Chapter 3	Restyled Pony, 1967–1968	31
Chapter 4	Shinoda Pens a Winner! 1969–1970	41
Chapter 5	Last of Generation I, 1971–1973	49
Chapter 6	Generation II, Mustang II, 1974–1978	55
Chapter 7	Generation III Rebirth, 1979–1986	61
Chapter 8	A Fresh Face, 1987–1993	71
Chapter 9	Generation IV, 1994–1998	79
Chapter 10	The Edge Look, 1999 and Beyond	89
Chapter 11	Mustang Miscellaneous	97
	Sources	118
	Price Guide	119
	Index	129

ACKNOWLEDGMENTS

I am fortunate. Just as I was finishing up my days at college, the Ford Mustang came to market. I still remember all of the hype and suspense surrounding the introduction of this new car. And, when production began, it was not unusual to stand on any street corner in 1964 and watch a nearly never-ending and colorful parade of Mustangs.

I have never owned a Mustang—yet—but like so many others, I have always wanted to! I found the next best thing to owning a Mustang car was collecting Mustang memorabilia.

For me, collecting is like owning a piece of a Mustang. I have been collecting Mustang memorabilia since the 1960s, and today, dozens of neat things still somehow find their way back home to become part of my collection.

Fortunately, I had more than just my own resources to glean in the preparation of this book. A special thank you must go to Paul McLaughlin, Wayne Moyer, my son John Coulter, Bill Bozgan, and Pete Hoyt. They allowed me unlimited access to their collections which, when added to mine, gave me an enormous assortment of items to consider. Thanks, guys, I couldn't have done it without you.

Additional photography was an essential part of completing this piece of work. Bob Downie, Paul McLaughlin, Keith Harrelson, and Pitkin Studio provided images that would have been particularly difficult for me to acquire.

I also want to thank companies who worked with me by sending items for me to photograph or images of their products for consideration: The American Highway, Taxor, Racing Champions/Ertl/AMT, and Revell-Monogram.

Some accomplished model builders honored me by submitting examples of their work. Each of the built-model Mustangs is considered very rare collectibles in any book. Thank you to Tim Boyd, Kenny Collins, Wayne Moyer, Paul Grala, Ed Sexton, and Tom Creeger who all offered me their best work.

Finally, thanks to Steve Hendrickson who gave me the opportunity to work on this challenging and enjoyable project.

Introduction

Provocative Pony

M-U-S-T-A-N-G! For some people, this two-syllable, seven-letter word conjures up visions of wild stallions on the Western plains, or images of a fast, powerful, and victorious World War II American fighter aircraft. For many of us, the Mustang evokes passionate visions of freedom and excitement, and the rumbling sound of a powerful V-8 engine in the open-air offering a spirited afternoon cruise on a winding country road.

After nearly 40 years, this latter description has become one of Ford's most popular cars. It has truly become a uniquely American icon; much more than the dwindling wild horses of the West or the dwindling fighters of the sky.

Ford's chief designer, John Najjar, is officially credited with naming the Mustang. Although his life-long fascination with the P-51 World War II fighter resulted in that original suggestion, the company's marketing research showed that most people thought of cowboys, Western plains, and wild horses when the word Mustang was mentioned. Thus, the "galloping horse" grille emblem was developed.

In that same time frame, Ford CEO and President Henry Ford II failed to consummate the purchase of Ferrari when Enzo Ferrari backed out at the last minute. Some believe Mustang's emblem was an "in-your-face" to Ferrari's legendary prancing stallion emblem.

When it was finally developed, Mustang actually was introduced twice in 1964. A wide-eyed public got a firsthand look at the new phenomenon at the New York World's Fair. Although it was technically a 1965 model, Ford managed to manufacture a few just in time to be selected as the official pace car for the Indianapolis 500 in April 1964. Legendary driver A.J. Foyt won his second Indy 500 and took home the new Mustang pace car as part of the bounty of his triumph.

Starting in early 1964, Ford's clever pre-introduction marketing hype raised the general public's anticipation to near fever pitch. The new Mustang was rolled out to eager Americans on April 17, 1964, at the New York World's Fair, and it quickly became the best-selling automotive nameplate in history at that time. There were over 22,000 orders on the first sales day, and nearly 700,000 total sales by the end of the 1965 model year. It took just two years for Ford to produce and sell 1 million Mustangs. It took Chevrolet 40 years to sell the same number of Corvettes. The brainchild of Ford Division General Manager Lido "Lee" Iacocca and his band of inspired engineers and designers was an instant hit and created a whole new genre in the American lexicon pony car.

It was unquestionably Ford's brilliant advertising campaign that whetted so many appetites for this new kind of car. The objective was to reach as many people with "the message" as quick as possible. Included in the corporate master game plan was a huge print-media conference for American newsstand staples including *Time, Newsweek, Life*, and *U.S. News & World Report* magazines. The company organized a test session for a select list of nearly 100 prominent reporters that featured a chance to drive the new Mustang from New York City to Detroit, Michigan. Over 10,000 Mustang media kits were distributed to a wide variety of magazines and newspapers here and abroad. Ford had seemingly thought of everything. There were even foreign language versions distributed in Europe.

Ford began airing short, quick-moving television commercial teasers that gave viewers just a fleeting glimpse of the new phenomenon, and took full advantage of the fact that Americans are so visually

King-K Products produced these resin/metal 1/3rd scale replicas of the original AMF 1965 Mustang pedal car. Limited to only 1,000 pieces per color (red, yellow, and white), these one-of-a-kind miniature replicas were originally sold through the Blue Diamond Classics Company.

The beginning and the end…so far! Shown is a pair of 1/25th scale Ford Mustang promotional models (a white 1964 1/2 and dark blue 1996) produced by AMT for new car promotional purposes. There has not been an annual Mustang promotional produced since the mid-1990s.

oriented. The media blitz came on April 16th, as a steady bombardment of Mustang television commercials premiered the day before the formal introduction on the three major broadcast networks, ABC, NBC, and CBS.

During this official Mustang introduction and advertising campaign, it was estimated that more than 4 million Americans hit their local Ford dealer show rooms for a closer look at the new car. Many customers signed up on the requisite waiting list; some eager buyers did so even without taking a test-drive.

In the first full week after the official introduction, four-color images of new Mustangs were featured in full-page advertisements in more than two dozen national magazines and more than 2,500 newspapers. Ford scrambled to set up Mustang displays in many high-traffic areas including major airport concourses, large retail shopping areas, and highly visible commercial business lobbies. Ford managed to virtually blanket the entire country with Mustangs.

The Mustang was recognized as a work of art by the likes of the upper-crust Tiffany & Co. This caliber of recognition added to the high-style image of the Mustang. The car was recognized for "Excellence in American Design" from Tiffany & Co. The award inscription read, "Mustang has the look, the fire, the flavor of one of the great European road cars. Yet it is as American as its name and as practical as its price."

From its inception, Mustang has always been known as a dependable, affordable car that could be equipped with uniquely personal features. Buyers have always been able to configure their Mustang in almost unlimited ways, allowing the car to become every person's ride. It virtually ensured that no Mustangs were exactly alike.

Interest in Mustang plastic model kits remains high. Shown is a current three-kit offering from Revell (No. 85-6861) which includes a 1993 SVT (Special Vehicle Team) Cobra, a 1969 Mach I, and a 1996 SVT Cobra convertible in 1/25th scale, all in one box.

The standard and optional equipment list in mid-1964 ranged from simple transportation to serious muscle. You could order your econo-Mustang with a six-cylinder engine and an automatic transmission, or turn it into a hairy-chested brute with over 270 horsepower, a race-tuned suspension, and four-on-the-floor!

Since April 1964, the Mustang has paced the Indianapolis 500, scored hundreds of racing victories, and recorded numerous championships on racetracks, both here and overseas. Mustangs have been featured in many high-grossing movies and popular TV shows. One special Mustang, a 1967 convertible, is owned by former U.S. President, William Jefferson Clinton.

Over the years, as interest in the car continued to expand, the "Mustang Madness" phenomenon fed a collectibles frenzy. Mustang T-shirts, jackets, jewelry, sunglasses, ball caps, key fobs, metal and plastic toys, and plastic model kits continue to be quickly gobbled up by eager enthusiasts.

Collecting memorabilia as a hobby is a popular and time-honored activity. People are known to amass collections of clothing items, political buttons, matchbooks, knives, cigarette lighters, postage stamps, DVDs and videotapes, and the list goes on. Ford Mustang enthusiasts collect everything and anything Mustang. Just as with other collectible enthusiasts, Mustang collectors may narrow their interests and only collect plastic kits and dealer promotional models, certain diecast models, and dealer sales literature, books, magazines, or printed display advertisements. Some of these items are already pretty pricey, especially when you consider that some items are nearly 40 years old.

With practically every new movie, kid's television show, or electronic game release, a wide range of merchandise hits the market with uncanny timing to take maximum advantage of the direct tie-in. Whether it's a toy in a Happy Meal at McDonalds or a special "Peanuts" NASCAR racecar model, the associated product sales often rival the dollars earned by the movie, television show, or electronic game. Many look to the original Mustang marketing and advertising blitz as ground zero—the moment it all started.

This book takes a close look at the nearly 40 years of Mustang cars and collectible models, organized by common body style within each generation. Model categories are broken down by 1964 1/2 through 1966, 1967 and 1968, 1969 and 1970, 1971 through 1973, 1974 through 1978, 1979 through 1993, and 1994 to the present. In the succeeding chapters, plastic, cast-resin and white metal model kits, diecast cars, dealer promotional models, children's toys, and slot cars of various scales are examined.

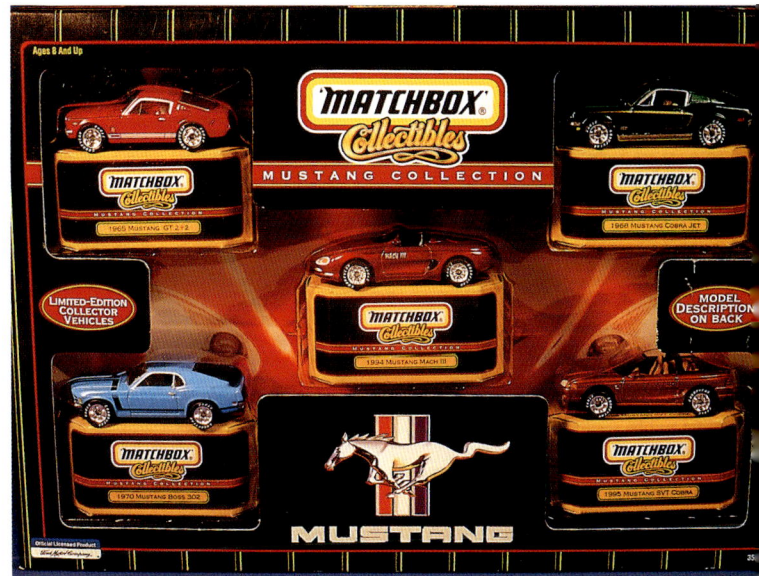

Shown is a five-car set of 1/64th scale diecast Mustangs from the Matchbox Collectibles series. Included is a 1965 2+2, a 1967 Cobra Jet, a 1994 Mach III, a 1970 Boss 302, and a 1994 SVT Cobra convertible.

In the final chapters, we take a close look at such memorabilia as Mustang apparel, postcards and trading card sets, whisky decanters, hat and lapel pins, jewelry items, and even Mustang Christmas tree ornaments and a go-cart. There is not room to show every collectible Mustang item ever made, but, hopefully, you will be pleasantly surprised (and pleased) with the contents of this book.

There are many items here that will interest not only the "strictly stock" Mustang enthusiast, but the Mustang race fan and the specialty Mustang lover as well.

There is liberal usage of words such as Cobra, Mach I, and Boss presented with legendary names such as Shelby, Saleen, Titus, Jones, Kendall, and Force. No matter what source of Mustang paraphernalia is your passion, you will find collectibles in this book to surprise and delight your taste.

As we move further into this new millennium, who would have guessed that the first American pony car may ultimately be the lone example that is still in production of this once dynamic and crowded pony car product category. It appears that the old and new Mustangs will be with us for some time to come, along with the thousands of desirable Mustang collectibles that continue to be coveted by enthusiasts worldwide. Whatever your chosen Mustang obsession, you will delight in these found objects of Mustang.

Three Mustangers

Ford Mustang enthusiasts are a loyal and eclectic group. Mustang car owners and collectors of Mustang paraphernalia are very often one and the

Plastic model kits of Mustang Indy 500 pace cars have always been a popular subject and prized by collectors. Shown are three Revell-Monogram Mustang pace cars including a 1964 kit No. 2456, a 1994 kit No. 2975, and a 1979 kit No. 2250.

Carroll Shelby created a special kind of magic when he created the first series of GT350s. Many manufacturers have produced scale replicas in a wide variety of scales and materials. Shown are a 1/20th scale by Revell Collection, a 1/32nd scale slot car by Carrera, and a built model (from a white metal kit) in 1/43rd scale by Precision Miniatures.

same. I have rarely encountered a person with a stash of Mustang collectibles who didn't own a Mustang or really long to own one. Conversely, I've never known a Mustang owner who didn't have at least a few collectibles. The following Mustang enthusiasts explain this point best in their own words.

Paul McLaughlin had been a loyal and dedicated Mustang enthusiast almost since the day the car hit the show room floor.

"My dad brought home a brand-new turquoise Mustang coupe the day of introduction, April 17, 1964. He took the whole family for a ride, cruising around town," McLaughlin said. "I was so taken by the car that I've been a Mustang loyalist ever since." McLaughlin feels that Mustangs have always had a certain magic about them and calls it "Mustang spirit." He believes it's what has kept Mustang ahead of the competition and the sole surviving pony car.

As for collecting Mustang paraphernalia, McLaughlin said, "The first piece of Mustang memorabilia that started my collection was a plastic "Dollar Mustang" dealer promotional model that I ordered from an advertisement in a car magazine. My dad

Miniature Mustangs continue to come in all sizes, shapes, and materials. This more than 3-inch-long cast-marble-look 1967 2+2 is the work of Marble Mountain Creations in Georgia. The approximately 8-inch-long cast-resin 1983 LX coupe came from Daytona Beach Trophy Co. and is made to resemble treated wood. The 1964 Mustang glass after-shave bottle is from Avon.

Being selected as the Indianapolis 500 pace car is an important and hallowed part of the Mustang mystique. These are diecast models of the three Mustang Indy pace cars. Clockwise: Brooklin 1/43rd scale 1964 Mustang Indy pace car; Jouef 1/18th scale 1994 Mustang Indy pace car, and a Johnny Lightning 1/64th 1979 Mustang Indy pace car.

gave my mother a similar model as a present. Mine was red and my mother's was white. I played with mine until it was virtually destroyed, mother put hers away for safekeeping. In 1984, shortly before she died, my mother gave me her Mustang promo. I value that model more than any of the hundreds of Mustang items in my collection."

Wayne Moyer's first new car was a sparkling, factory-fresh 1964 1/2 Poppy Red convertible. The pony mystique, and considerable pre-introduction marketing hype wasn't lost on this aeronautical engineer. According to Moyer, "On April 17, 1964, I skipped college classes, and waited at the front door of my local Ford dealer until he opened." That first Mustang purchase led to the purchase of others, including a 1989 GT convertible. Moyer thinks Mustang owes its longevity to sticking with the same recipe since the beginning. "It's a simple formula: good looks, excellent performance, and a laundry list of standard and optional features that allow you to tailor the car to your personal tastes. An excellent racing record hasn't hurt the prowess and performance image of the Mustang either."

Moyer considers his most valued collectible to be his full-size 1989 GT convertible. Of the more maintenance-free Mustang items, he puts a high value on his Brooklin 1968 1/43rd Carroll Shelby signature version of a dark green GT350. "Only a little more than 200 of these were ever made and given as contest prizes by Model Expo—who knows how many survive today," added Moyer. "I've only seen four of them in the last 25 years of collecting Mustang paraphernalia."

John Coulter is a first-time Mustang owner at age 32. Coulter admitted to lusting after a 'Stang since his junior high days. "I had a friend with a 1969 Mach I and I really liked that car. I began taking serious notice of the first 5.0-liter GTs in 1982 and 1984," Coulter said. "I really got hooked on the 1984 SVO Mustang and the Hi-Po 302 1985 Mustang GT."

Coulter thinks Mustang has endured over time and outlived its competitors mainly because of its conservative styling and consistent quality. "The Mustang has always had a more conservative, 'brutish' look, unlike the 'boy racer' styling of its competition," Coulter said.

For John Coulter, his most valued Mustang collectible is a resin hand-built 1/43rd scale All Sport Trans-Am Mustang model of the car Tommy Kendall drove to 11 straight victories in 1997. There are fewer than 100 of these models built by Peter Wingfield at Pro-Line Miniatures. During that record-breaking season, Coulter met Kendall for the first time at the Mid-Ohio Sports Car Course. Kendall won that race on his way to breaking the long-standing, season victories record of the late Mark Donohue.

With Mustang enthusiasts and collectors, it all comes down to one conclusion: the cars, the owners, and the collectibles are constant. As you move through the pages of this book, you will fully appreciate this focused intensity; the pride of ownership for a nearly limitless array of Mustang items available throughout the last 40 years. Saddle up and head 'em out as we get up to a full gallop on the trail of some of the most valued Mustang collectibles. Some are old, some are new, and some are clearly priceless.

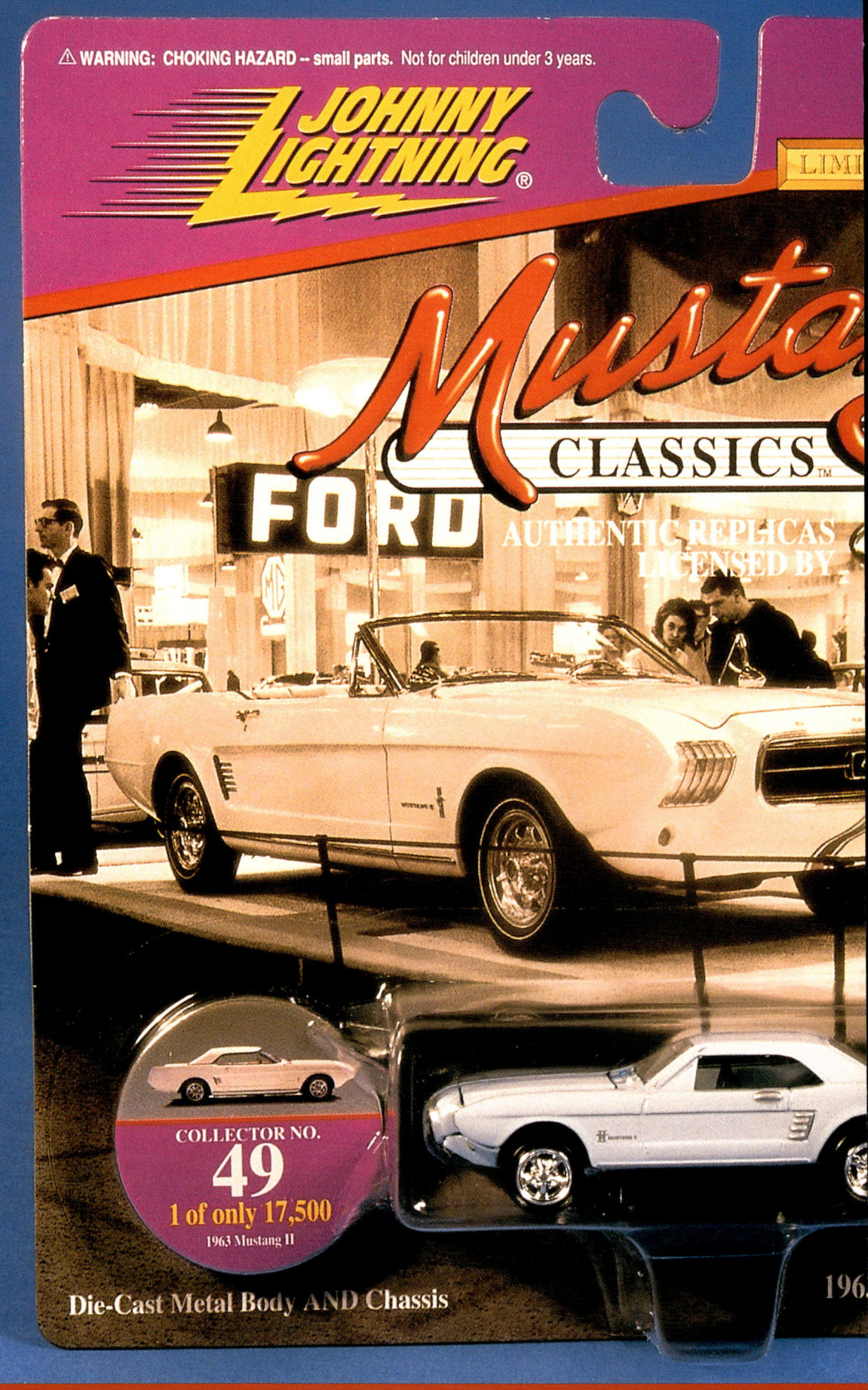

CHAPTER ONE

CONCEPTS AND SHOW CARS

Since the invention of the automobile in the late nineteenth century, car enthusiasts have been fascinated by sporty, grand-touring-style vehicles. Be it a hopped-up Ford Model T, Stutz Bearcat, Auburn 851 Boattail Speedster, Lincoln Continental, MG-TD, Jaguar XK-120, or a Chevrolet Corvette. Most of these cars have unfortunately shared many common maladies. Most specialty marques were quite expensive and only available in small quantities. Plus, they weren't very practical and didn't offer much flexibility in options or pricing.

In the post–World War II United States, we were able to enjoy a few sporty, personal cars such as the Chrysler Town & Country, Ford Sportsman, Kaiser Darrin, and the legendary two-seater Ford Thunderbird. The Chevrolet Corvette, although rather expensive and only a two-seater, eventually rose to world-class status and popularity. By the end of the 1960s, there was a void in the marketplace that begged to be filled for many car enthusiasts.

After the introduction of the revolutionary, yet highly controversial, Corvair in the fall of 1959, Chevrolet produced a performance version of the Monza to catch their competitors (i.e., Ford) off guard. While Ford's Falcon—a direct rival to the Corvair—was aimed squarely at utilitarianism, Chevrolet cranked out their sporty, four-passenger Monza coupes and convertibles by the thousands. Even with the advent of the brand-new lightweight,

Johnny Lightning's Playing Mantis line, made by Polar Lights, offers this 1/64th scale diecast of the 1963 Ford Mustang II. So far, there are no other known plastic or diecast examples of the Mustang I or II.

13

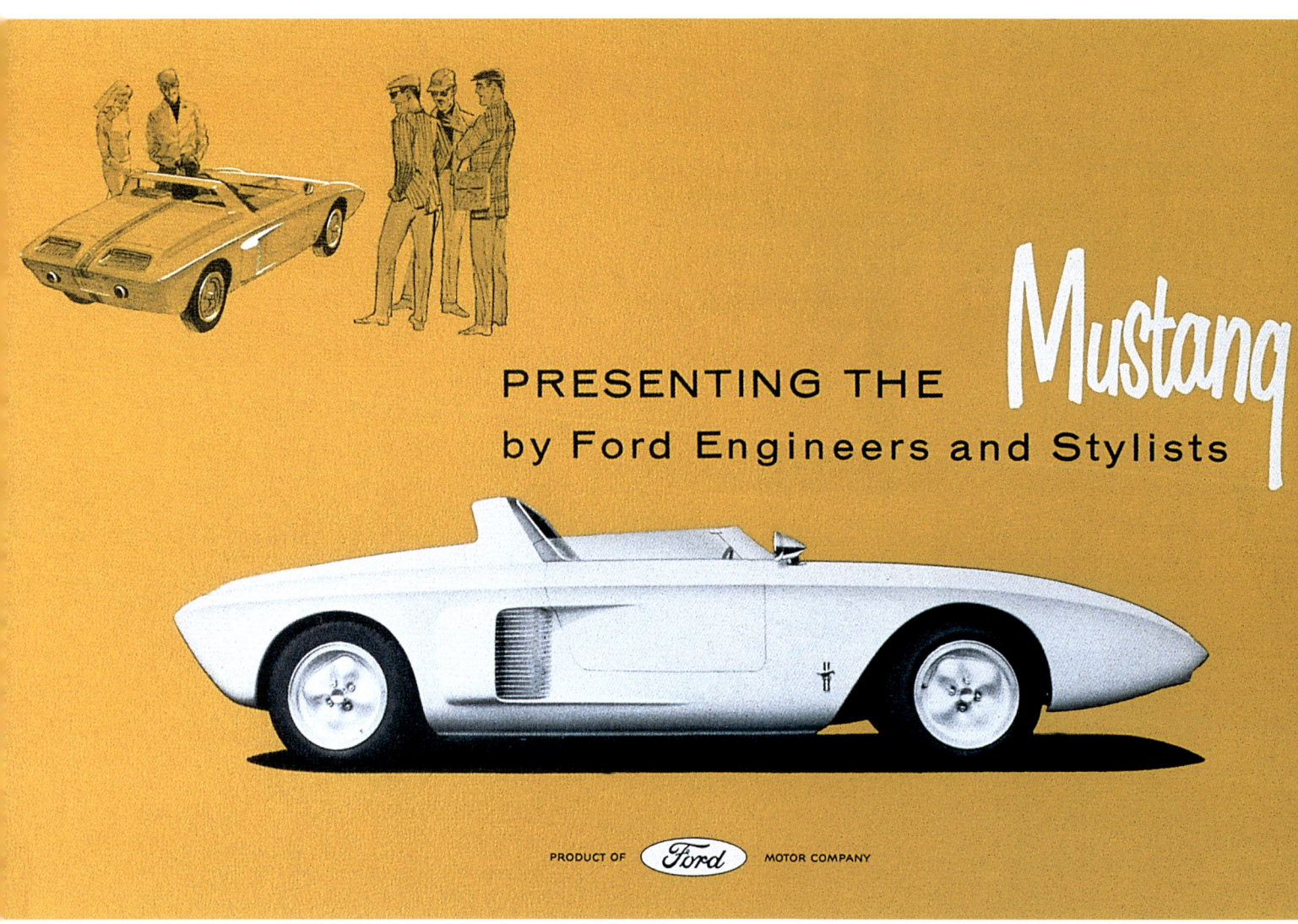

Shown is an example of one of the 20,000 postcards handed out to spectators by Ford officials at the U.S. Grand Prix at Watkins Glen, New York, in the fall of 1962. The piece measures 10 3/4 x 6-1/2 inches. The contents lists all technical specifications for the two-seater including engine, brakes, frame, body shell, and transaxle, showing assorted black-and-white images. The folder is lithographed in yellow and white. Collector Paul McLaughlin managed to acquire this piece even though he was a long way from Watkins Glen in 1962.

small-block V-8 for the Falcon, Ford dealers complained about nearly non-existent sales. A reasonably priced, sporty performance car was needed fast.

In 1960, Lee Iacocca replaced Robert McNamara as head of the Ford division at Ford Motor Company. From the time he spent working under McNamara, Iacocca had learned quickly to catalog each and every one of his ideas, and always construct a thorough paper trail in support of any significant concepts. As though the stars and planets were in complete alignment, everything converged at one point in time for Iacocca. He had one notation in his notebook of ideas that envisioned a low-priced, sporty car that might conceivably be based on existing parts and technology.

Iacocca methodically petitioned the company president, Henry Ford II, on the idea. Once he received approval from Henry (and a $40 million budget), Iacocca set a series of events into motion to assemble the best talent within the corporation to create a new kind of car, utilize current technology, and promise a base price under $2,500!

In search of the automotive Holy Grail, 13 full-scale design studies were done by late 1961, code-named Allegro. By mid-1962, public and corporate interest had switched to the unique two-seater concept car named the Mustang I.

The nimble little mid-engine roadster debuted at the 1962 U.S. Grand Prix at Watkins Glen, New York. The sleek two-seater, V-type, four-cylinder sports car zipped around the Finger Lakes' area road course and reached more than 120 miles per hour with legendary racecar driver Dan Gurney at the wheel. Company representatives handed out more than 20,000 brochures about the Mustang I. Public interest was very high, especially after Ford showcased the

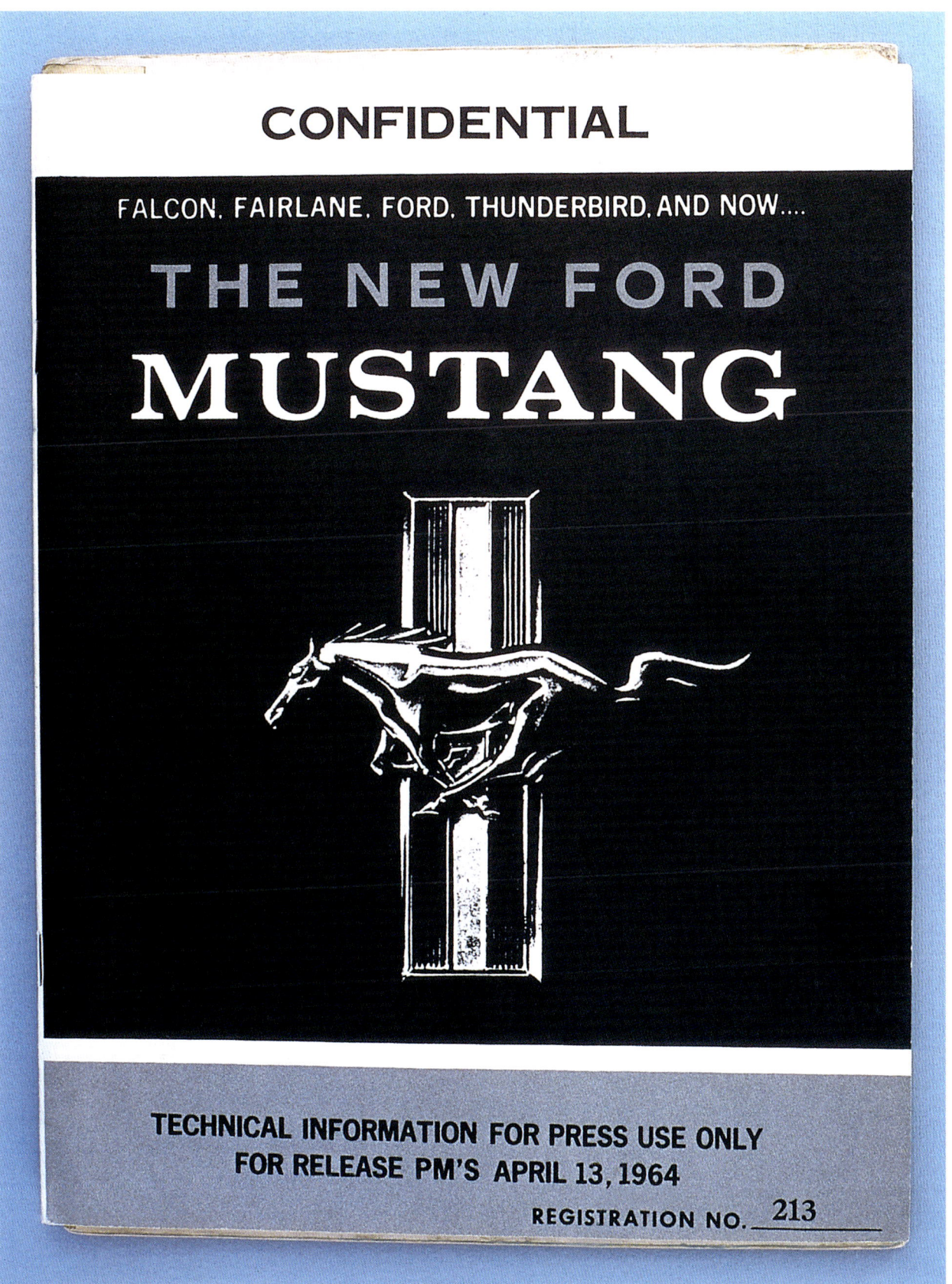

It was unquestionably Ford's brilliant advertising campaign that whetted so many appetites for this new kind of car. The company's main objective was to reach as many people with "the message" as quick as was humanly possible. Included on the corporate playlist was a huge print-media conference for American newsstand staples such as *Time, Newsweek, Life*, and the *U.S. News and World Report* magazines. The company organized a test session for a select list of nearly 100 prominent reporters that featured a chance to drive the new Mustang from New York City to Detroit. Additionally, over 10,000 Mustang media kits (like the example shown here) were distributed to a wide variety of magazines and newspapers here and abroad. Ford had thought of everything. There were even foreign language versions distributed in Europe. Note that the cover is numbered and marked confidential. An original piece like this is absolutely essential to the serious Mustang collector.

Shown are two 1/25th scale plastic model kits of the 1963 Ford Mustang II. At left is Lindberg kit No. 72169 and at right is the original version by Industro-Motive Company (IMC) kit No. 109. Ironically, both kits are produced from the same original IMC tooling.

new concept at hundreds of college campuses from coast to coast. There was every indication that the car was a big hit, but Iacocca remained convinced that there wasn't a large enough market for a car that only had room for two people.

By 1963, Ford designers and engineers, with substantial prodding from Iacocca, had created what would become the production Mustang. It featured seating for four, and used a boatload of existing and well-tested Falcon and Fairlane parts and assemblies. This near-final version established Mustang-exclusive design cues that remain part of the marque to this day. The galloping horse grille emblem, concave side scoops, and the three horizontal taillights define the Mustang.

It was decided a new show car was needed to pacify the public fervor. Iacocca intended to create a unique one-off show car to mask the actual Mustang's production appearance to buy more development time. The Mustang II was actually a pre-production version that Ford had sent to the Detroit Steel Tubing custom shop. The Mustang II featured revised front and rear fascia panels and the appearance of a chopped top. The new creation only served to further whet the appetite of an already eager car-buying public.

The stage was now set for the official public introduction of the much-anticipated Ford Mustang, thanks to the media hype, pre-introduction marketing and sales strategy, and thorough focus group polls. Iacocca bet the farm and his entire future in the industry by splitting Mustang production to three assembly plants. Some pundits within Ford projected initial sales of 20,000 to 40,000 units the first year. Iacocca sharpened his pencil and suggested they should set sales projections much higher, to 250,000 units. Thankfully, for all those involved in the Mustang effort, nobody at Ford could really anticipate the rocket ride that lay ahead.

The fledgling plastic model car kit industry was already positioned to take off like a rocket when the introduction of the Ford Mustang in April 1964 helped light the fuse. Suddenly, the hobby of collecting and building models was really hip. The first unassembled polystyrene Mustang kit in 1/25th scale came from a small company, Industro-Motive

This built version of the Mustang II is the handiwork of Kenny Collins. Note that the original and reissue kits contain a few additional items of interest. Also shown with the built model and the kit box is a Mustang key ring that was included with the kit.

Corporation (IMC). IMC's first kits in late 1964 were in 1/32nd scale. Their first 1/25th scale release was the original Ford Mustang II show car.

That first Mustang kit (No. 102) was novel, but never garnered the interest with collectors like the production-based kits from AMT and MPC. Part of that limitation may have been the kit's complexity because it featured opening panels and delicate, steerable front suspension assemblies. In the late 1970s, IMC joined Lindberg and Testors, Inc. to form the RPM Corporation. In 1996, Lindberg reissued the old IMC Mustang II kit as item No. 72169. The Lindberg and IMC releases are both produced from the same original IMC tooling from the 1960s. The original IMC kit today is valued at 12 to 15 times more than the newer Lindberg version. The only other model of this significant Mustang is Polar Lights' Johnny Lightning's Playing Mantis 1/64th scale diecast 1963 Ford Mustang II.

There are a few very desirable Mustang collectible products from this pre-production era that remain popular with many collectors. Included on that short list would be one of the original 10,000 media press kits distributed just prior to introduction. One of the foreign language versions of the press kit would be a real find. Specific original issues of popular national magazines like the April 17, 1964, *Newsweek* and *Time* are also quite collectible. Both magazines featured Lee Iacocca on their covers that week. Any original magazine featuring the new 1964 1/2 Mustang on the cover is desirable. A big plus would also be considerable editorial space devoted to the Mustang in the magazine.

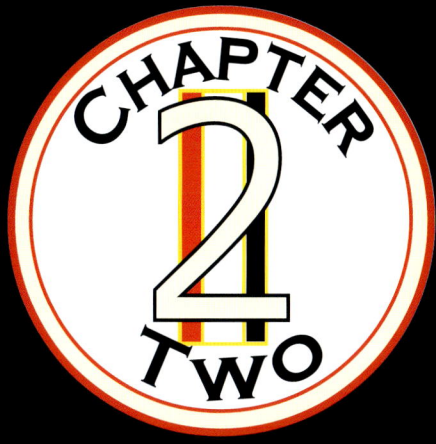

CHAPTER TWO

GENERATION I BEGINS, 1964½–1966

Certainly Mustang got a lot more than its 15 minutes of fame when it was introduced to the public twice during the spring of 1964. There were thousands of very receptive future customers who received an initial up-close-and-personal look at the "next new thing" at the New York World's Fair. The second time was just a few short weeks after the official introduction when the Indianapolis Motor Speedway selected Mustang as the official pace car for the 1964 Indianapolis 500. Four-time winner A.J. Foyt scored his second victory in the storied event and received the official Mustang pace car as part of his bounty.

Motor Trend magazine awarded its prestigious Car of the Year award to the Ford Motor Company in early 1964. The final decision was supposedly based on Ford's commitment to a competition-testing program, and the Galaxie, Fairlane, Falcon, and Thunderbird were specifically cited in the magazine. Unquestionably, the *MT* staff was strongly influenced by their inside knowledge of the upcoming Ford "Corvette fighter," which was thought to be named Torino. A short three months later at the New York World's Fair, the Mustang was unveiled to instant popularity and booming sales.

It's hard to find a pristine example of this rare 1964-1/2 Mustang pedal car that was manufactured by AMF Corporation. It was originally sold through Ford dealerships for $12.95. Today this piece can bring nearly 40 times of that amount.

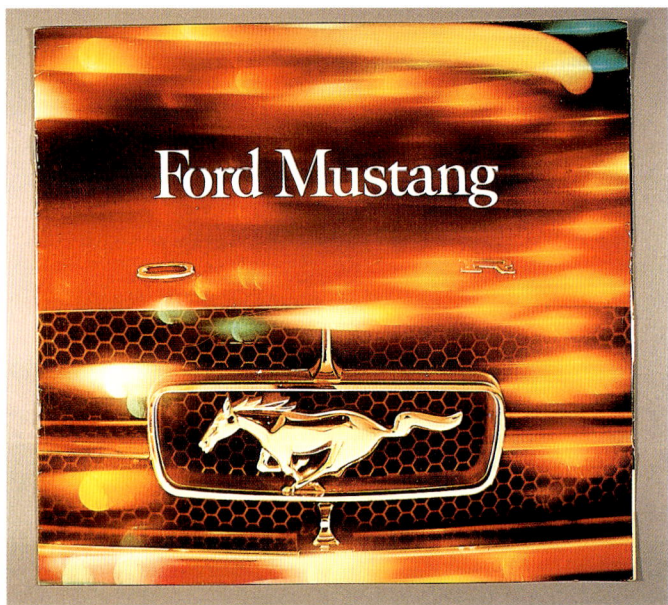

Shown is the front cover of the very first production Ford Mustang dealer sales brochure. This is a particularly sought-after and highly collectible piece of automotive literature.

This pair of 1964-1/2 Mustang 1/25th scale models was produced by AMT as promotion items for Ford. At left is the standard "notch-back" coupe in blue. At right is the very rare Indy 500 pace car promo.

As soon as the Mustang was officially introduced, it didn't take long for an estimated 4 million car-hungry Americans to descend on their local Ford dealers for a more personal experience with the new car. There were many potential buyers who eagerly added their names to a long waiting list. A few overzealous customers bought new Mustangs without even so much as a spin around the block! One buyer even slept in a car in the dealer show room to wait for the bank approval of his loan application!

The first production Mustangs rolled off the Detroit-area assembly line on March 9, 1964. The goal was to see that each of Ford's more than 8,000 franchised dealers had at least one Mustang on the premises prior to the April 17th unveiling.

When production got into high gear, 100,000 units rolled off the line that first month. The 250,000 cars produced before the World's Fair intro still fell short of the customer demand. Eventually, three plants (Detroit, Michigan; San Jose, California; and

Shown is a trio of original Mustang promotional models made by AMT in 1/25th scale. From left: a red 1966 coupe, a red 1965 2+2, and a Wimbledon White 1964-1/2 coupe.

Three different hobby kit manufacturers produced unassembled 1/32nd scale plastic kits of the first-generation Ford Mustang. All of these model kits are of the 2+2 body style. On top is the AMT version kit No. 7111. At left is Monogram's version of a 1965 Shelby Mustang, kit No. 2000. At right is the Revell, Inc. version, kit No. 1250. Although the box art depicts a 1966 Mustang, the model is actually a 1967 body style. The AMT and Monogram kits are molded in white, and the Revell model is molded in light metallic green.

One of the few large Mustang kits is the 1/16th scale from AMT. The kit was first issued in 1979 as kit No. 4804. The same kit was reissued again in the early 1980s as kit No. 7508, and again in 1984 as kit No. 6722.

Shown are three 1/25th scale, 1965 Mustang plastic model kits. At bottom left is the original 1964-1/2 Mustang model kit by AMT, No. 6154. At the top is AMT kit No. T-157 "High Roller" depicting an altered wheelbase drag car. Kit tooling for the original 1965 Mustang was permanently modified to produce this version. At right is AMT kit No. T-180, a 1965 Mustang-bodied, modified tube-frame dirt track stock car racer. This item does not share any parts or pieces with other Mustang kits.

Metuchen, New Jersey) had to be assigned to build nothing but Mustangs to keep up with the onslaught.

Between March 1964 and December 1965, nearly 750,000 cars were produced. By March 1966, 1 million cars had gone to satisfied customers. In just 33 months, Ford had produced nearly 1.5 million Mustangs. By the end of Generation I (1964-1/2 through 1966), Ford Motor Company's Mustang profits topped $1 billion.

The very first production Ford Mustang, a Wimbledon White convertible, was sold to airline pilot Stanley Tucker. Mr. Stanley traded his prized possession back to Ford Motor Company in 1967. That first 1964 1/2 Mustang now resides in the Henry Ford Museum in Dearborn, Michigan.

Mustang Production Figures
April 1964 through 1965: 680,989
1966: 607,569

Shelby Mustang GT350 Production Figures
1965: 561
1966: 2,378

Motorsports Mustang I

The Mustang not only set all kinds of production and sales records, but also racing quickly became a strong part of its pedigree. In early 1964, Mustangs showed their real potential as racecars. Alan Mann and his associates in Europe built cars to compete in the Tour de France. The Mustang cars, driven by Brits Peter Harper and Peter Proctor, finished first and second to win, and handily dominated their class.

By 1965, the Ford Motor Company was making really big noise in worldwide motorsports in places including Le Mans, Watkins Glen, Indianapolis, Daytona, and Bonneville. Ford racecars were very

Drew Hierwarter built this dirt track 1965 Mustang from AMT kit No. T-180.

Here are three examples of AMT 1/25th scale plastic 1996 Mustang model kits. At top is an original kit No. 6156 that could be built as a hardtop or convertible. At bottom is an original kit No. 6166 with the 2+2 body style. At right is kit No. 2254 from the Crusin' USA series that was molded in green plastic. This version was created from the original promotional model tooling and was first released in 1977 as kit No. 2207.

Here is a pair of 1/24th scale Monogram kits of early Shelby Mustangs. At top is a 1966 GT350 H kit No. 2736 molded in black plastic. Carroll Shelby's company built the full-size cars for Hertz Rent A Car. At bottom is kit No. 2700 of the original 1965 GT350, molded in white plastic.

Shown is an unbuilt Monogram kit No. 2700 of the 1965 Shelby Mustang. The author built the 1966 Shelby Mustang in the foreground using Monogram kit No. 2797 and Fred Cady Design decals.

active in NASCAR Grand National stock car racing, the U.S. Auto Club (USAC) open-wheel circuit, the Indy 500, and Formula One and World Sports Car racing. Mustangs were quickly in the thick of things! The Mustang set speed records on the Bonneville Salt Flats; in International Hot Rod Association (IHRA), American Hot Rod Association (AHRA), and National Hot Rod Association (NHRA) drag racing; in the 12 Hours of Sebring sports car race; in European and Mexican rallying; and in Sports Car Club of America (SCCA) road racing.

In the NHRA's Factory Experimental (A/FX) drag racing class, the 1965 Mustang 2+2s equipped with single overhead cam (SOHC) 427 monster V-8s gave the competition all that they could handle. Ford's corporate race shop, Holman-Moody, built 10 of these rocket ship ponies. Bill Lawson, in the Tasca mount, scored a decisive victory the first time out. Drivers including Les Ritchey, Gas Ronda, and Dick Branson made their reputations at the wheel of these high-speed Mustang missiles.

This is one of the very few remaining plastic model kits that was sold in a collectible tin box. This is the Revell-Monogram 1965 Mustang in 1/24th scale kit No. 85-4157.

23

Shown is a pair of Revell-Monogram 1/24th scale plastic model kits of the 1965 Mustang. At bottom is the 2+2 kit No. 2713 that was released only once in 1985. At top is the Hertz GT350 H, most recently reissued in 1996.

When Sonny and Cher were at their zenith in the mid-1960s, custom car building czar George Barris designed this pair of special ponies for the duo. Simultaneously, the original AMT kit No. 907-170 was released, only once, in 1966.

Carroll Shelby, the 1959 LeMans 24 Hour winner and father of the Shelby Cobra, was consulted by Iacocca for ideas that would give the Mustang a real performance image. The legendary Shelby Mustang GT350 and GT350R evolved from those meetings. Although the GT350 was really a racecar with license plates, the R model was the "genuine article" created specifically to compete in the SCCA series. Mark Donohue, Jerry Titus, and Bob Johnson drove 1965 Rs to national titles. The GT350Rs also won the SCCA B-Production titles for three straight years.

In 1966 NHRA Funny Car competition, Holman-Moody built eight fiberglass-bodied Mustangs on a Logghe tubular chassis with a fuel-injected SOHC race-prepped V-8 for competition. Bill Lawson, Phil Bonner, Dick Branson, Gas Ronda, and Hubert Platt won a boatload of national events and high-profile match races with these vehicles.

Initial Generation I Mustang production figures were very impressive even without any direct competition. However, all of that would change for many decades starting with the 1967 model year.

Mustang I Collectibles

There are probably more desirable Mustang collectible items from the original body style (1964-1/2 through 1966) than any of those that followed. It is probably due to the icon status of that original pony car. Simply put, when most people visualize a Ford Mustang, even people who have only a passing interest, they visualize that original Generation I shape.

The most desirable, expensive, and treasured original dealer sales literature to collect is from the first few years. Since hundreds of thousands of pieces were printed and distributed during that initial production phase, one may assume it would be plentiful and therefore cheap and easy to find. What makes these items so valuable is the fact that they were never created with an eye toward collectibility. Dealer sales literature has always been produced for the sole purpose of promoting the purchase of a new Mustang. The greater percentage of those original brochures most likely wound up in the garbage. It is a diminishing supply driven by increased demand. It's a simple economic equation. More people want the literature from the early years, which there is less and less of.

Monthly magazine display advertisements are popular Mustang collectibles. This product type will never be prohibitively expensive. Most collectors remove the ads from popular automotive magazines of the time including *Car Life, Motor Trend, Car and Driver, Road & Track,* and *Hot Rod.* Other more mainstream monthlies such as *Look, Life,* and *Saturday*

This trio of Monogram 1/24th scale plastic model kits represents the wide variety of subject material that the manufacturer was able to produce from one basic tool. Shown clockwise: kit No. 2456, issued in 1995; a racing GT350R kit No. 2969, issued in 1994; and the original-issue 1965 GT350 kit No. 2700, from 1985. All three kits were cast in white plastic.

Evening Post are a few of the numerous places such things are usually found.

There are dozens of examples of miniature Generation I Mustangs created in promotional and diecast models; plastic kits; and plastic, cast-metal, and tinplate toys in a wide variety of shapes, sizes, and scales. The original Mustang promos and plastic kits top the list with many exceeding the $200 mark value-wise. The first unopened, unassembled Mustang 1/25th scale kits by AMT (and later from MPC) are today worth more than 15 times their initial retail selling price.

Unique Generation I collectibles include such diverse products as the AMF pedal car, Aurora HO slot cars, and Japanese tinplate toys. The AMF 1965 Mustang pedal car once sold at the local Ford dealer for less than $15. Today, any example in original, pristine condition is valued at nearly 15 times that price. An Aurora Thunder Jet HO scale slot car sold

Shown is an original AMT 1965 1/25th scale slot car kit. This item features a hard plastic body, which is actually an AMT promotional shell.

25

Aurora was a major player in HO scale slot car racing models in the mid-1960s with their Model Motoring series of cars, slot car tracks, and accessories. Shown is Aurora's 1965 Mustang 2+2 HO slot car model with its original packaging.

Shown is a trio of Post Cereal 1966 Mustangs; these were premium items offered in cereal boxes. The series included a coupe, convertible, and 2+2 body styles measuring 3 inches in length. The F&F Mold and Die Works in Dayton, Ohio, made these small ponies that were cast in pastel shades of yellow, blue, green, and red.

for under $10 when new, but today it can bring over $100 in excellent condition. What makes these items so valuable is that they were originally produced to be used. Many were raced and not collected, and that's why when you find one in like-new condition, deep pockets are essential. Everybody wants a collectible that shows no signs of use. Japanese tinplate toys, static or battery operated, remain very popular to Mustang memorabilia collectors. Original products from companies such as Bandai often approach the $200 to $300 mark for like-new condition pieces.

These are examples of early Shelby Mustangs in three different scales. Left to right: Revell's Creative Masters 1/20th scale 1965 Shelby Mustang, Precision Miniatures 1/43rd scale white metal 1965 Shelby, and a Carrera 1/32nd scale 1966 Shelby slot car model.

This set of five, 1964 Mustang Indy pace car diecast models represents four different scales and five different manufacturers. The replicas shown include the 1/12th scale by Ertl, the 1/18th scale by Revell in 1993, a pair of 1/43rd scale models by Brooklin and Precision Miniatures in the 1980s, and the recent 1/64th scale for the Polar Lights Johnny Lightning line.

Lane Automotive produced this pair of 1966 Shelby Mustangs in 1/18th scale. At left is their GT350 in Candy Apple Red. At right is their replica of Cristi Edlebrock's GT350R vintage racer. "Carroll Shelby," like "Mustang," has become a common household name. The former Texas chicken farmer and world-class sports car racer, turned mundane Mustangs into aggressive street machines and bona fide fire-breathing racecars.

This quartet of first-generation Mustang diecast convertibles includes: a 1/18th scale by Revell; a black 1/32nd scale Speedy Power toy (found in many gift and specialty shops); a red 1/64th Matchbox that was produced as a premium for *Toy Cars and Vehicles* magazine; and a recent 1/64th for the Polar Lights Johnny Lightning line.

King K Ltd. Company makes these miniature 1964-1/2 Mustang pedal cars. They are exact replicas of the original AMF full-size version made between 1964 and 1971.

This set of five, 1964-1/2 red Mustang convertible diecast models represents as many different scales and manufacturers. The replicas shown include a 1/12th scale by Ertl, a 1/18th scale from the Precision 100 Collection by Racing Champions, a 1/24th scale by The Franklin Mint, a 1/43rd by Brooklin, and a recent 1/64th by Johnny Lightning.

CHAPTER THREE

RESTYLED PONY 1967–1968

Ford Motor Company sold nearly 1.3 million Mustangs during April 1964 through September 1966. With those whopping sales numbers, what could they possibly do for an encore? Ford was busily preparing for the 1967 model year with a fresh take on the original pony car. After all, there was this wonderful thing called competition!

Ford was well aware, early on, that General Motors could not ignore the Mustang for long and would respond with two pony cars of its own. Ford also realized a major restyling of their highly successful car would be a risk, but it was one they would have to take due to direct competition joining the market.

For 1967, Mustang received an entirely new body shell, but it retained many distinctive design cues. The car continued to ride on a 108-inch wheelbase and retained some of the same basic driveline pieces from the first installment. The new Mustang looked more aggressive, rounder, and fuller with a much more muscular appearance.

Love those diecast 1968 Mustangs whatever size or scale. Shown is a quartet of 1968s in different scales by different manufacturers. From left: the limited-production 1/18th scale Ertl Taska Ford Super Stock drag car, the Revell-Monogram Bullitt 1968, the current 1/43rd scale Brooklin 1968 GT, and the Johnny Lightning 1/64th scale GT 2+2.

AMT produced a series of promotional models for different car makes for 1967 that included the Mustang GT 2+2, shown here. These factory-assembled replicas are pricey and scarce, according to today's collectors.

Plymouth introduced its Barracuda two weeks prior to the Mustang's introduction in the spring of 1964. The 'Cuda never did prove to be much of a threat to the 'Stang. The real competition would come from General Motors. GM was finally able to see daylight after it sat on the sidelines while Ford mopped up with its new sales leader. In 1967, Chevrolet and Pontiac introduced their own pony cars in an attempt to deliver a one-two punch to the segment leader. The Chevrolet Camaro and Pontiac Firebird, although variants on common chassis and driveline components, did not share the same exterior sheet metal. Both cars had distinctly individual styling.

Camaro sold 220,917 units, and Firebird sold 82,558 units in 1967. Both models came back in 1968 to do 243,095 and 87,112, respectively. Without question, these two GM sporty cars—sales numbers combined—cut into Mustang sales, which sold 610,794 units in 1967, and 321,855 units in 1968. The GM siblings combined in 1968 to just barely outsell Mustang for the first time, especially since the Ford entry fell to nearly half the sales of the year before.

The list of Mustang competitors increased again in 1968. AMC brought the Javelin and AMX to the market. Due to a highly restricted budget, both AMC pony cars were much more than siblings. The AMX was a shortened-up version of the Javelin, which allowed AMC to boast it made the "other" American two-seater sports car as Corvette had held the sole distinction.

Carroll Shelby continued to provide Mustang lovers a juiced pony that for 1967 featured very distinctive exterior design treatments. The 1967 Shelby Mustangs carried revised front fender extensions,

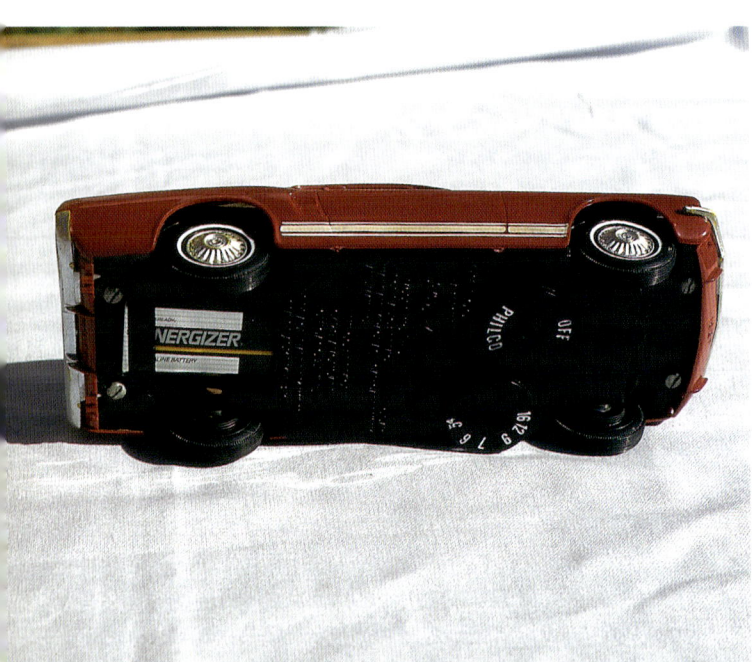

This is the underside of an AMT 1967 Ford Mustang portable AM radio. This example, though more rare, for some reason is a less desirable collectible than the friction-powered or standard promotional versions.

Shown is a pair of 1/25th scale 1967 Mustang plastic model kits. At top is an AMT kit No. 6631, first issued in 1995. At bottom is an original AMT 1967 Mustang 2+2 kit No. 6167.

32

This is a 1/16th scale 1968 Shelby Mustang GT500 plastic model kit manufactured by the Japanese company Nichimo. This item, kit No. MC1601-3500, was first issued in the 1980s.

Here are two examples of 1/25th scale AMT plastic model kits of Shelby Mustangs. At top is a 1967 GT350 kit No. 6633, first issued in 1995. At bottom is a 1968 GT500 kit No. T-397, first issued in 1968. This particular model is a 1974 reissue.

Shown is a Shelby Drag team 3-in-1 AMT kit from 1970. This 1/25th scale kit No. 501 includes a 1969 Ford Galaxie, a tandem axle trailer, and a 1968 Shelby Mustang GT500.

There were popular songs recorded about Mustangs including Wilson Pickett's classic, Top 40 hit "Mustang Sally." This is AMT's 1/25th scale 1968 Shelby Mustang kit No. T-296 (original kit box and built model), the very first replica of the marque. Included was a small vinyl-on-cardstock 33-1/3 rpm record with authentic "snake" sounds and an auditory E-ticket ride in the car with Carroll Shelby doing the driving that was music to every Mustang enthusiast's ears!

A close-up look at the vinyl-on-cardstock record from AMT 1968 Shelby Mustang kit No. T-296.

and an aggressive grille cavity with two inboard driving lights. A kicked-up tail with a pronounced spoiler and sequential taillights at the rear (borrowed from the Ford Thunderbird) set the tone. There was now a new big-block GT500 to join the legendary GT350 in the Shelby line. For 1968, Shelby Mustang production moved from California to Michigan as Carroll Shelby's business interests had moved on to more pressing matters involving other Ford products.

Motorsports Mustangs

Mustang continued to make headlines in motorsports in both 1967 and 1968. "Ohio" George Montgomery drove his Malco Mustang to the NHRA AA/Gas championship. Tom Grove won the Spring Nationals title in a Mustang. In the SCCA Trans-Am series, Jerry Titus won the driver's title in a Shelby Mustang, while Ford Motor Company recorded their second manufacturer's championship.

With Wilson Pickett's smash hit "Mustang Sally" on the Top 40 charts in 1968, Ford introduced the 429 Cobra Jet (CJ) as a performance option on the Ford

The author built this replica of a 1968 Shelby Mustang from AMT kit No. T-296 when it was first released in 1968.

pony car. Monster-motored 'Stangs, built by the likes of Bill Stroppe in California and Holman-Moody in North Carolina, recorded many Super Stock victories in NHRA drag racing. The 1968 'Stang retained a great deal of the appearance of the brand-new 1967. The visual change was minor and concentrated primarily on the grille and side scoop trim. The startling drop in Mustang sales for 1968 set the stage for a second round of "freshening" for the 1969-1970 model years. Ford was hoping that a revised exterior combined with new performance models and driveline options would see Mustang well ahead of the competition once more.

Mustang Production Figures
1967: 472,121
1968: 317,404

Shelby Mustang Production Figures
1967: 3,225
1968: 4,451

Shown are 1/25th scale plastic model kits of two specialty show cars from Ford. At top is the Autolite Special Hi-Performance Mustang kit No. T-147, first issued in early 1969. At bottom is the Mach I concept car kit No. 2148 that was first issued in 1967. Ironically, both kits are based on the same 1966 Mustang show car.

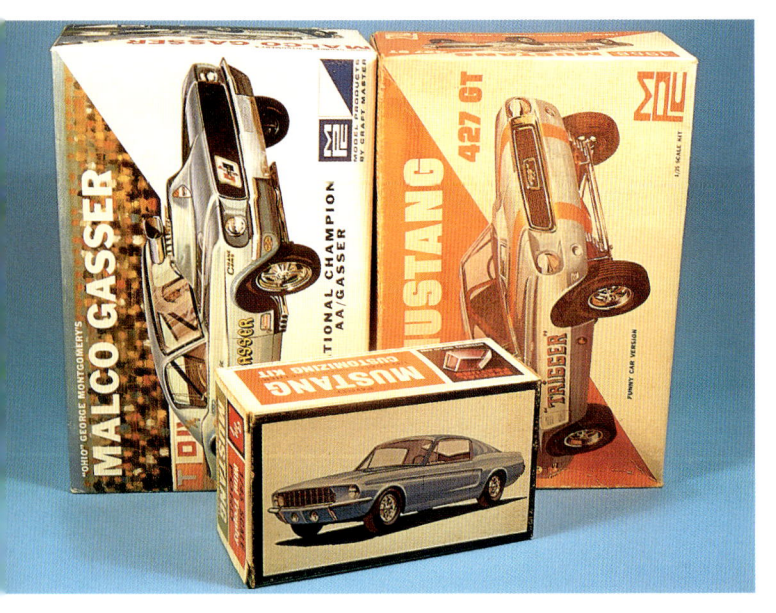

Shown is a trio of Mustang plastic model kits in two different scales. At the foreground is an AMT 1968 custom Mustang in 1/43rd scale kit No. M-793. At left is MPC kit No. 0704, The Malco Gasser, AA/Gas 1967 Mustang. At right is MPC kit No. 1368, a 1968 Mustang GT 2+2 annual.

Here is a trio of 1/25th scale 1968 Shelby Mustang plastic model kits by AMT, all from the same tooling. At bottom left is the original issue from 1968 of kit No. 296. At bottom right from 1974 is reissue kit No. T-397, and at top is a reissue kit No. 6541 from 1986.

Here is a trio of 1968 Mustang plastic model kits by AMT. At bottom right is the original issue of the 1968 Shelby Mustang kit No. T-296. Bottom left is the reissue of the same kit No. 2215 from 1979. At top is a 1/43rd scale stock 1968 Mustang GT 2+2 kit No. 3577.

36

The first Mattel Hot Wheels line included this 1968 Mustang. This remains an expensive and highly sought-after Mustang collectible today, and commands a healthy price.

Shown are two examples of AMT 1/25th scale plastic model kit No. 6168, a 1968 Mustang GT 2+2. The custom-built version in the foreground is the work of Tim Boyd.

Mustang Collectibles

The total redesign of the popular pony car continued to spawn a plethora of collectible items in many dimensions and materials. Mustangs continued to be featured in display advertisements and as cover material on popular automotive magazines. Dealer sales literature, and promotional and plastic model kits remain highly sought-after materials among the original annual items either produced to promote or immortalize the 1967 and 1968 Ford Mustangs. Original Mustang sales literature in pristine condition also commands high prices among collectors.

AMT, Revell, and MPC were among the domestic manufacturers making plastic kits in 1967-1968. AMT manufactured a variety of factory-built plastic models in 1/25th scale including friction-powered, promotional, and those equipped with a 9-volt battery-powered AM radio.

Three 1967 Ford Mustangs are shown in two scales. The metal Bullitt Mustang is in 1/25th scale. The two 1/43rd scale diecast 1967s in the foreground are by Matchbox, which is now owned by Mattel.

Mattel's Hot Wheels automotive diecast line has long been known for its bargain-priced 1/64th scale products. Of late, this California-based company has expanded into much larger scales. Shown are their large and small 1967 Shelby Mustangs from the Legends series. They are 1/24th and 1/64th scale replicas.

From the Ertl 1/43rd scale diecast Class of 1967 is this three-car set featuring a 1967 Shelby Mustang between its two primary competitors that year, the Camaro and Firebird.

In this same time period, diecast makers such as Mattel got in the act by including Mustang models in their Hot Wheels line. AMF continued with their large 1/12th scale efforts and produced a second battery-powered Mustang in the form of a 1967 GT 2+2.

The 1967-1968 body style Mustangs, especially the fastback 2+2, presently remain a favorite model for replica and toy makers.

With the advent of a restyled Ford Mustang for 1967 and 1968, both AMT and MPC responded with newly tooled 1/25th scale plastic kits. Unlike the previous variety of body styles, both manufacturers' offerings were of the fastback 2+2. No kit of the convertible or notch-back coupe versions has been produced in kit form to date. Neither AMT kit No. 6167 nor MPC kit No.13 have ever been reissued. The original AMT 1967 kit tooling was likely updated and modified to make the 1968 Shelby GT350 kit No. T-296. This is also true for the MPC offering, which was updated to a 1968, and then again to a 1969 version. There are many elements that contribute to the current value of these original annual kits, but it is mostly the fact that the old tooling does not currently exist.

Today, both AMT and Revell-Monogram have filled in the gaps for builders and collectors, alike. AMT generated new tooling for the 1967 Mustang GT kit No. 6631 and the 1967 Shelby GT350 kit No. 6633, and re-released the models in 1994 and 1995. Both releases are based on the same basic tooling. It's unlikely these kits will ever achieve the status of original releases.

There's nothing more eye appealing for a collector than the sight of four 1967 Shelby Mustangs in a row! Shown from left: Ertl's American Muscle 1/18th, Mattel's Hot Wheels 1/24th, Ertl's 1/43rd, and the 1/64th version from Mattel's Hot Wheels Legends series.

With the phenomenal growth in interest in 1/18th diecast in the early 1990s, AMT-Ertl has produced a number of 1967-1968 Mustangs in their American Muscle series. These releases have included both street-stock versions and selected items including limited-production drag cars such the Taska Ford, a popular and victorious vintage Super Stock drag car driven by Hubert Platt; and the famous "Dyno" Don Nicholson 1968 Super Stock Mustang. These were all well-executed products that will fit nicely into any miniature Mustang collection, but it may be many years before they are considered rare collectibles.

The 1/12th scale plastic and stamped metal 1967 Mustang GT 2+2 produced by AMF, and the battery-operated 1967 Mustang 2+2 Japanese tinplate toy will continue to be sought after and valuable simply because of their nostalgia, and because they have not been produced for more than 35 years—and likely they never will be again. If you purchased these things when they were new, as Mustang owner and collector Paul McLaughlin did, the extent of the accrued value of his collection becomes very apparent. The AMF 1967 model originally retailed for just $5.95 from the local Ford dealer. Today, this item is valued at approximately 100 times that original price.

This battery-operated 1967 Mustang 2+2 Japanese tinplate toy measures 10 inches long. This item was made by Bandi of Japan. The body shell is metal, but the hood is made from clear plastic. The V-8 engine lights up when the electric motor is running.

Gone but not forgotten. The British manufacturer Brooklin created this pair of 1/43rd scale diecast 1968 Shelby Mustangs. In the background is the hand-signed version, which was part of a special Model Expo promotion. Reportedly, approximately 200 pieces were manufactured, which makes this one of the rarest of Mustang collectibles. In the foreground is the standard version that was offered for sale to the public until Shelby lodged a licensing complaint with the company. Afterwards, the tooling was converted to a regular 1968 Mustang GT 2+2.

This 1/12th scale plastic and stamped metal 1967 Mustang GT 2+2 was produced by AMF as a marketing tool for Ford dealerships. At more than 16 inches long, this is the largest replica of this body style pony made to date. The plastic body-hinges at the front reveal a stamped metal chassis that housed the battery-powered motor that drove the rear wheels. Once it was activated, the headlights, taillights, and instrument panel operated, and the model could run forward or reverse and be set to follow a circular path. The corrugated shipping box even served as a garage. All this sold for only $5.95 in 1967, batteries included.

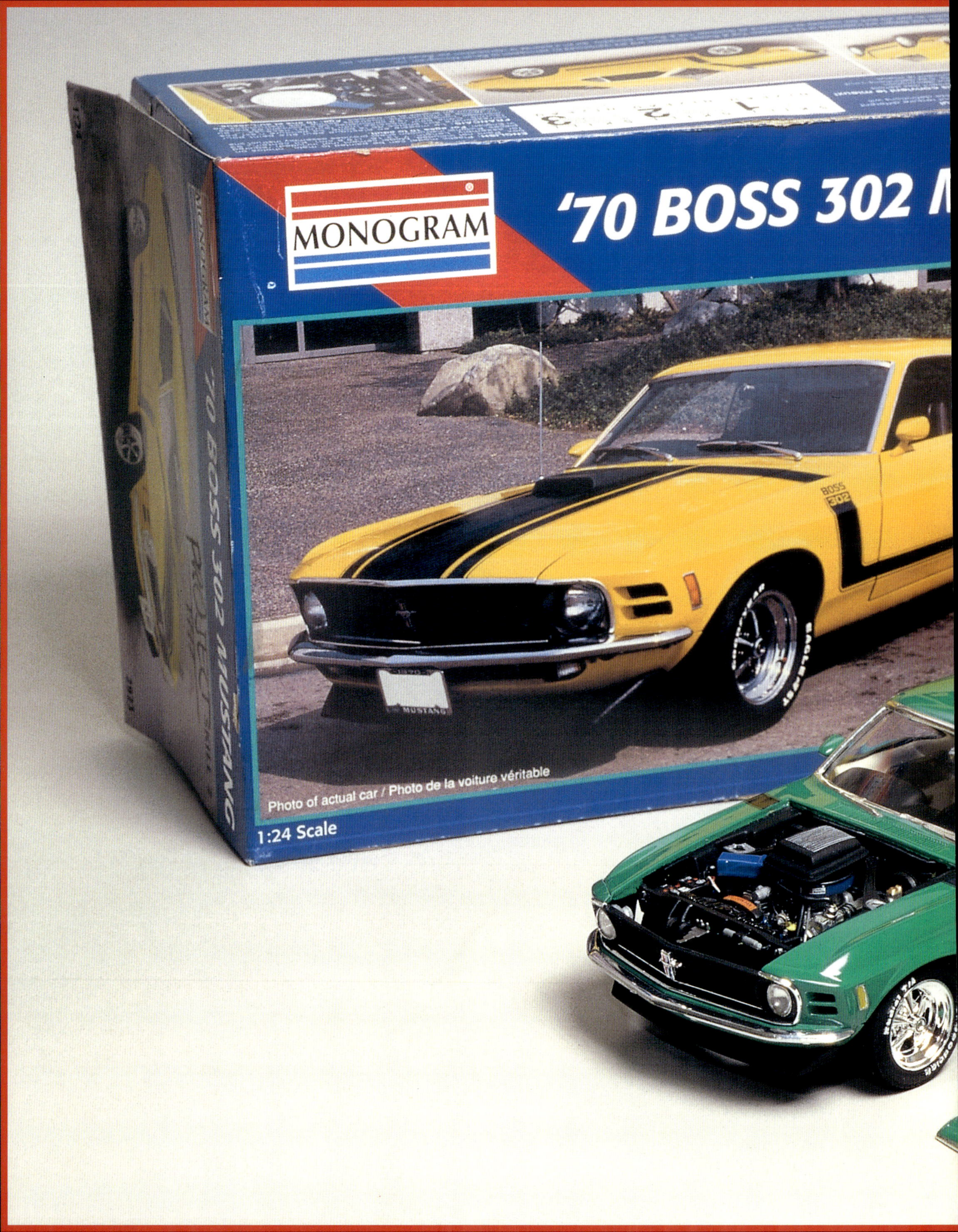
MONOGRAM
'70 BOSS 302 M
Photo of actual car / Photo de la voiture véritable
1:24 Scale
'70 BOSS 302 MUSTANG

CHAPTER 4 FOUR

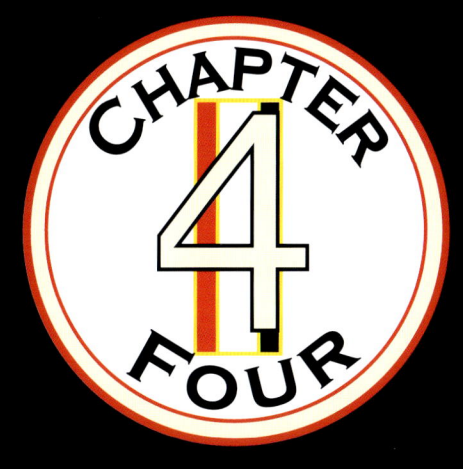

SHINODA PENS A WINNER! 1969–1970

Chevrolet Corvette designer Larry Shinoda eventually came along as part of the sweeping coup that brought former GM senior executive Semon "Bunkie" Knudsen to Ford in the late 1960s. One of the new regime's first tasks at Ford was to quickly inject pizzazz into the whole Ford line. High on the list of priorities was to fuse some new life into an embattled Mustang, which now had a multitude of direct competitors. The Mustang received a major shot of adrenaline from industrial designer Larry Shinoda's pen for the 1969-1970 model year. The bold and style-setting body lines of the 1967-1968 Mustang became even more muscular, aggressive, and trendy with the new surface shapes for 1969-1970 from Shinoda's creative mind. Knudsen—who became president at Ford—and company certainly accomplished the mission, and helped create one of the most stylish and mechanically influential automotive product lines of the era.

Legendary model names such as Boss, Mach I, Ram Air, Cobra Jet, and Grande were added to the lengthy Mustang pedigree in 1969. Some pundits claim Larry Shinoda's application of the term "Boss" to various Mustang image-building performance models was because he always referred to Knudsen

These are the kit box and built version of Monogram's 1970 Mustang Boss 302 kit No. 2923. The built version is the handiwork of Tim Boyd.

AMT produced this rare and valuable promotional version of the 1969 Mustang fastback. The model is in 1/25th scale, and was only produced in red. It was quite difficult to find when new.

Here is a trio of 1969 Ford Mustang 1/25th scale model car kits from three different manufacturers. Top center is a Revell Mach I kit No. 7121, initially issued in 1989. At left is an original annual AMT Mach I kit No. Y905. At right is a reissue of an MPC Mach I kit No. 1-0731 that was available in 1985.

Shown are three popular plastic Ford Mustang model car kits. Top center is an MPC 1/25th scale 1969 Mr. Gasket Gasser (kit No. 725) replica of the one that was built and driven by "Ohio" George Montgomery. This kit was first released in 1970. At left is a Revell 1/24th scale 1969 Shelby Mustang GT500 kit No. 7161, which was a new release in 1988. At right is an MPC 1/25th scale 1969 Mustang Super Stocker kit No. 1-2753, which was first available in 1970.

as "Boss." Whatever the case, the name became an integral part of the heady Mustang lexicon. The use of Mach, Ram Air, and Cobra Jet are pretty obvious considering the corporate effort that emphasized light speed, raw power, and snake-inspired propulsion. Grande (introduced in 1969) marked Ford's first concerted effort to establish a plush and upscale Mustang model—one that reeked of swank and didn't even offer the buyer most of the extra-cost performance-enhancing options available on virtually every other Mustang.

Driveline choices for 1969 were expanded to include some of the marques' most storied performance engines including the Boss 302, Mach I 428, and the Boss 429-cid V-8—the "King Kong" of all pony car versions. The venerable Hi-Po 289 was replaced with a new 302-cid small-block that dripped with high-performance, race-bred parts, and technology.

The Boss 429 was a different story. Never before—and it would probably never happen again—would a special Mustang be used by Ford to shoehorn its way into compliance with NASCAR homologation guidelines. The horsepower race was at a fever pitch with Ford and Chrysler slugging it out year after year with bigger and "badder" monster V-8s. Ford had developed their own version of a Hemi-head engine to compete with Chrysler's 426 "elephant" engine. A strict reading of the NASCAR Grand National rule book did not seem too specific on what particular production car a special engine had to be installed. Ford hired custom and specialty automotive builder Kar Kraft to squeeze the huge powerplant into approximately 900 Mustangs, thereby accomplishing two things at once: NASCAR approval for competition, and the creation of the Boss 429. There were 859 Boss 429s built for 1969, and only 499 rolled out for 1970.

Mustang sales continued to slide down the chart in 1969. Chevy Camaro sales alone rose to 243,095 units in 1969, but were still a few thousand shy of the segment leader. Although when combined with Pontiac Firebird's number of 87,708, the GM siblings moved ahead of Mustang once more on the sales charts.

In 1970, GM and Ford were locked in mortal combat over pony car turf. An economic slowdown, an impending energy shortage, and sky-rocketing insurance rates took a mighty toll on overall sales for

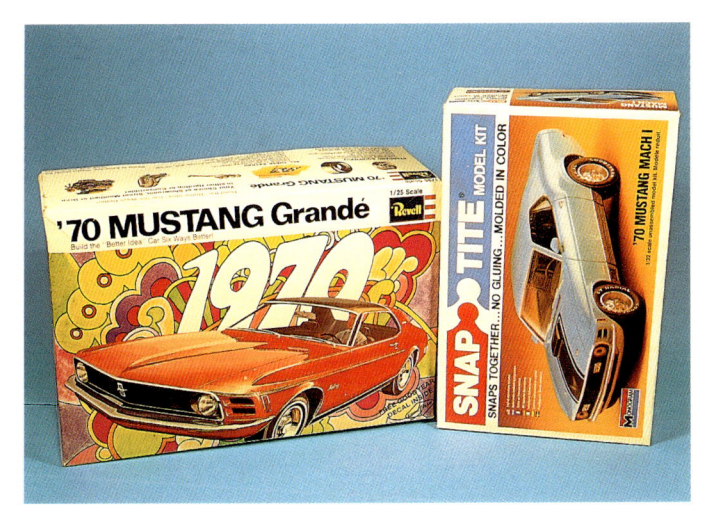

The 1970 Ford Mustang has been produced in plastic kits in a variety of scales. Here are two such examples. At left is an original annual issue 1970 Mustang Grandé in 1/25th scale, Revell kit No. H-1212. At right is a Monogram 1/32nd scale Mach I kit No. 1030, which was first available in 1981.

This is an original issue AMT 1/25th scale plastic kit of the Russ Davis long-nose drag racing Mustang Funny Car kit No. T-307. This AMT kit continues a long tradition of including a vinyl-on-cardstock phonograph record titled, "The Sounds of Drag Racing."

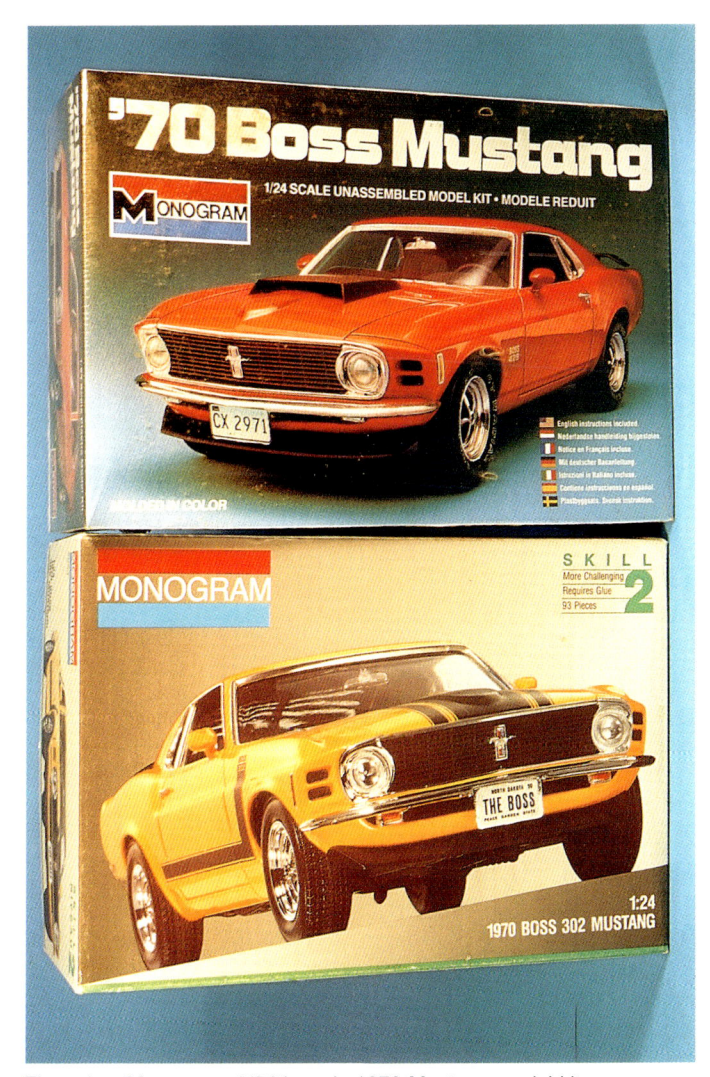

These two Monogram 1/24th scale 1970 Mustang model kits were produced from the same basic tooling. At top is a 1970 Boss 429 kit No. 2282, which was a new release in 1981. At bottom is a 1970 Boss 302 kit No. 2923, which was first introduced in 1991.

all competitors. Mustang sales dropped more than 100,000 units for 1970. Camaro and Firebird sales were hit even harder as their combined numbers (173,628) slid roughly 20,000 units below those for Mustang as the decade came to a close.

Ford Mustang Production Figures
1969: 299,824
1970: 190,727

Shelby Mustang, 1969-1970

The Shelby Mustang, which was now being built in Michigan instead of California, was about to run its course. It's quite difficult for anyone other than a true Mustang authority to tell the difference between a 1969 and a 1970 Shelby Mustang without checking the specimen car for telltale identification marks such as the VIN numbers and the factory paperwork. Factually, of the 3,153 1969 and 1970 Shelby Mustangs, 789 1969s that were unsold were actually re-titled as 1970s. There is virtually no difference between 1969 and 1970. Notably, the addition of dual black hood stripes and a Boss 302-style front spoiler on the 1970s were the only visual changes from 1969.

Shelby Mustang Production Figures
1969–1970: 3,153 (789 1969s were updated to 1970)

Motorsports Mustangs

Ford continued its Total Performance program on the street and in competition with the throttle wide open and running in high gear! In Bonneville speed trials Ford sent examples of the Boss 428 Mach I, Boss 429, and Boss 302. All-around racer Mickey Thompson, drag racer and Indy car driver Danny Ongias, and racer/magazine publisher Ray Brock set

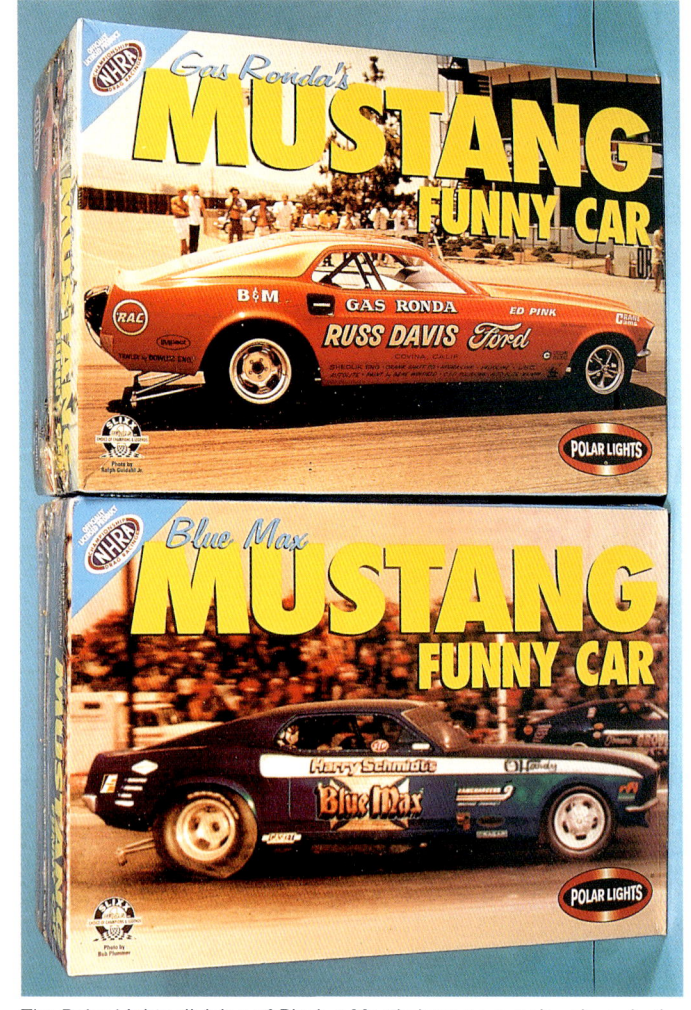

The Polar Lights division of Playing Mantis became a major player in the 1/25th scale plastic kit business in 2000. Shown are two examples of their Mustang drag racing Funny Car kits. At top is the Gas Ronda 1970 Mustang F/C kit No. 6056. At bottom is the Blue Max 1970 Mustang F/C kit No. 6507. For 2001, these kits were also produced with clear, see-through plastic body shells as part of Polar Lights' ghost series.

The level of detail on this 1970 Mustang Boss 302 is extremely realistic. This model was built by Tim Boyd.

Shown are two different 1/24th scale releases of Monogram's 1970 Boss 429 kit No. 2728 (left) and No. 2282 (right) plastic kits. This version of the 1970 Mustang Boss 429 was built by Tim Boyd.

295 USAC records with these Mustangs including one which was run for 24 hours over a 10-mile course at an average of 157 miles per hour!

In drag racing, Danny Ongias piloted his Mickey Thompson–built AA Funny Car Mustang to record speeds and numerous victories in 1969 and 1970. The competition continued to escalate in the SCCA Trans-Am series as Mark Donohue's Camaro just barely beat out Bud Moore's Mustangs for the cherished national title. In 1969 there were two Ford team efforts. Team Shelby fielded two cars with Peter Revson at the wheel. Bud Moore also ran two cars with Parnelli Jones and George Follmer sharing the driving duties.

For 1970, Bud Moore Engineering carried the factory banner alone for Ford and built Mustangs for Follmer and Jones once more. It paid dividends in spades as Parnelli won the driver's title over Mark Donohue by just one point. Ford Motor Company took the manufacturer's title once again.

In mid-season 1970, Ford Motor Company made the dramatic and sweeping decision to cut back its factory support of motorsports. After the 1970 season's triumphs, there were many years before a Ford factory presence was seen in NASCAR, NHRA, Trans-Am, or any other major-league racing venue.

Legendary stock car driver Dick Trickle continued the uphill battle in the early 1970s and raced a Mustang on Midwestern short tracks and recorded nearly 70 feature wins. Other stalwarts and diehard Ford devotees continued to go at it alone in racing. Famous competitors, such as Bob Glidden, "Dyno" Don Nicholson, and Shirley Muldowney represented Ford in specially built Mustangs in NHRA Pro-Stock and Funny Car competition in the early 1970s.

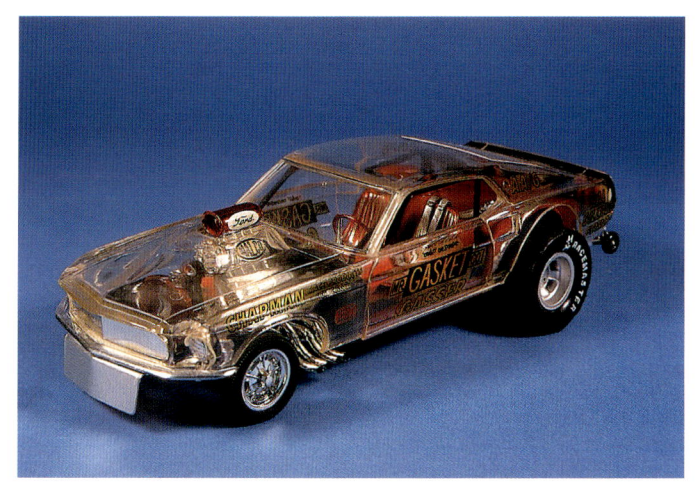

Kenny Collins built this replica of "Ohio" George Montgomery's 1969 AA/Gas Mustang drag car from MPC kit No. 0725. The clear body shell shows off the inner workings of the tube-frame racer.

Shown are two variations of the Ertl 1969 Mustang Mach I diecast in 1/64th scale. At left is the American Muscle version, and at right is the Ertl Collectibles version.

Mustang Collectibles

Although the variety and selection can't compare with the choices available for 1964 1/2 through 1966, there are a surprising number of interesting Mustang collectibles for the years 1969 and 1970. Dealer sales brochures remain near the top of the list among collectors. Special magazine inserts and unique dealer and trade show handouts are also tops on the list of paper Mustang collectibles for this era.

AMT, Revell, Monogram, and Lindberg all produced plastic model kits and promotion models of many of the body styles and model designations for the 1969 and 1970 'Stangs. Of course, the original annuals are the items of greatest value and most sought after by seasoned collectors today.

Many diecast manufacturers have gotten into the fray including Ertl/AMT, Mattel, Matchbox, and Polar Lights' Johnny Lightning line to produce miniature Mustangs from this era. In this medium you can find big, little, and midsize 1969-1970

This is a trio of very rare and sought-after Mebetoys 1/43rd scale 1969 Mustang Boss 302s. In the background is an example with its original display base from the Wayne Moyer collection. At left is another example of the Mebetoys Boss in almost pristine condition. At right is one restored by Moyer.

45

An excellent 1/64th scale 1970 Boss Mustang is included in this Hot Wheels 30th anniversary, 1970s Muscle Cars, four-piece set.

Four scales of miniature 1969 Mustangs make for a pretty picture anytime. Shown is a quartet that includes a 1/18th Ertl 1969 Mach I from the American Muscle series, a 1/43rd scale Sheriff's Cruiser by Road Champs, an Ertl 1/64th from the American Muscle series, and a 1/87th scale plastic replica from the Revell-Monogram Mini Exacts series that was released in 1988.

Mustangs in a wide variety of scales from 1/18th and 1/43rd to 1/64th. The Mach I, Boss 302, and even Shelby Mustangs are available in interesting factory colors and trim levels.

Mustang sales literature for 1969 and 1970 remain especially popular with collectors primarily due to the aggressive styling and successes in competition like SCCA Trans-Am and professional drag racing. The introduction of such legendary models of the Mustang at this time, such as the Mach 1 and Boss 302 and 429, provide the kind of enduring image that true legends are made of.

AMT produced what is the most rare, highly valued, and expensive promotional model to date. This model is in 1/25th scale, was only produced in red, and was quite difficult to obtain when new in 1969. It's not clear why there were so few models produced or why they were not widely distributed. I found mine through a collector/dealer at the time, and I paid $10 plus shipping. I must remind you that this was quite a bit to pay for a new promo, as the standard fare was more in the $3–$5 price range. Many collectors today value this single item at 120 times my original purchase price.

Popular Ford Mustang plastic model car kits in 1969 and 1970 included stock production and competition-inspired versions. The MPC 1/25th scale 1969 Mr. Gasket Gasser (kit No. 725) is a racing kit.

Here is a trio of diecast 1970 Mustangs in three different scales. From left: an Ertl Grabber Yellow 1970 Mustang Boss 302 in 1/18th scale, a 1/43rd scale Boss 429 by Matchbox, and a Hot Wheels Boss in 1/64th scale.

The Revell 1/24th scale 1969 Shelby Mustang GT500 kit No. 7161, was released in 1988. MPC also did a 1/25th scale 1969 Mustang Super Stocker replica kit No. 1-2753 that was driven by racing veteran Dick Trickle. Both kits were first issued in 1970, and command a price nearly 30 times original retail today.

One, if not the most collectible diecast Mustang model, is the Brooklin 1968 Shelby Mustang. This dark green 1/43rd "Carroll Shelby signature" GT350 is quite a rare piece. "Only a little more than 200 of these were ever made. Given as contest prizes by Model Expo, who knows how many survive today," said collector Wayne Moyer. "I've only seen four of them in the last 25 years of collecting Mustang paraphernalia."

Personally, I have refused a verbal offer of $2,000 for the model I own. Beyond this era, except for maybe a pair of early 1970s AMT promos in the $250 range, there are no "bank buster" Mustang collectibles.

By 1968 the "bloom was off the rose," as they say, for the Shelby Mustang. Carroll's interests had moved on to more pressing challenges. Production of the marque had moved in-house with Shelby Mustangs produced on a special assembly line in the "Motor City" instead of Shelby's California facility. In 1997, Ertl produced replicas of the 1969-1970 Shelby Mustang convertible in a couple of different color combinations. This red-over-black example is certainly a handsome piece. There is some debate on whether this combination was an actual production option.

WARREN TOPE
TRANS-AM MUSTA
amt
'73 MUSTANG
MACH I
STREET
MACHINES
•MOLDED
IN COLOR
•MOULÉ EN COULEUR
•FARBIG
VORGEFERTIGTE TEILE
1/25
MODEL KIT
MAQUETTE 71 PIÈCES
MODELL-BAUSATZ
MATCHBOX
1/25 SCALE CUSTOMIZING KIT WITH THREE B
'72 M
MACH I
DAN GURNEY
INVITES YOU TO ENTER THE
KIT IDEA CONTEST
of the FUN GROUP at
General Mills

CHAPTER FIVE

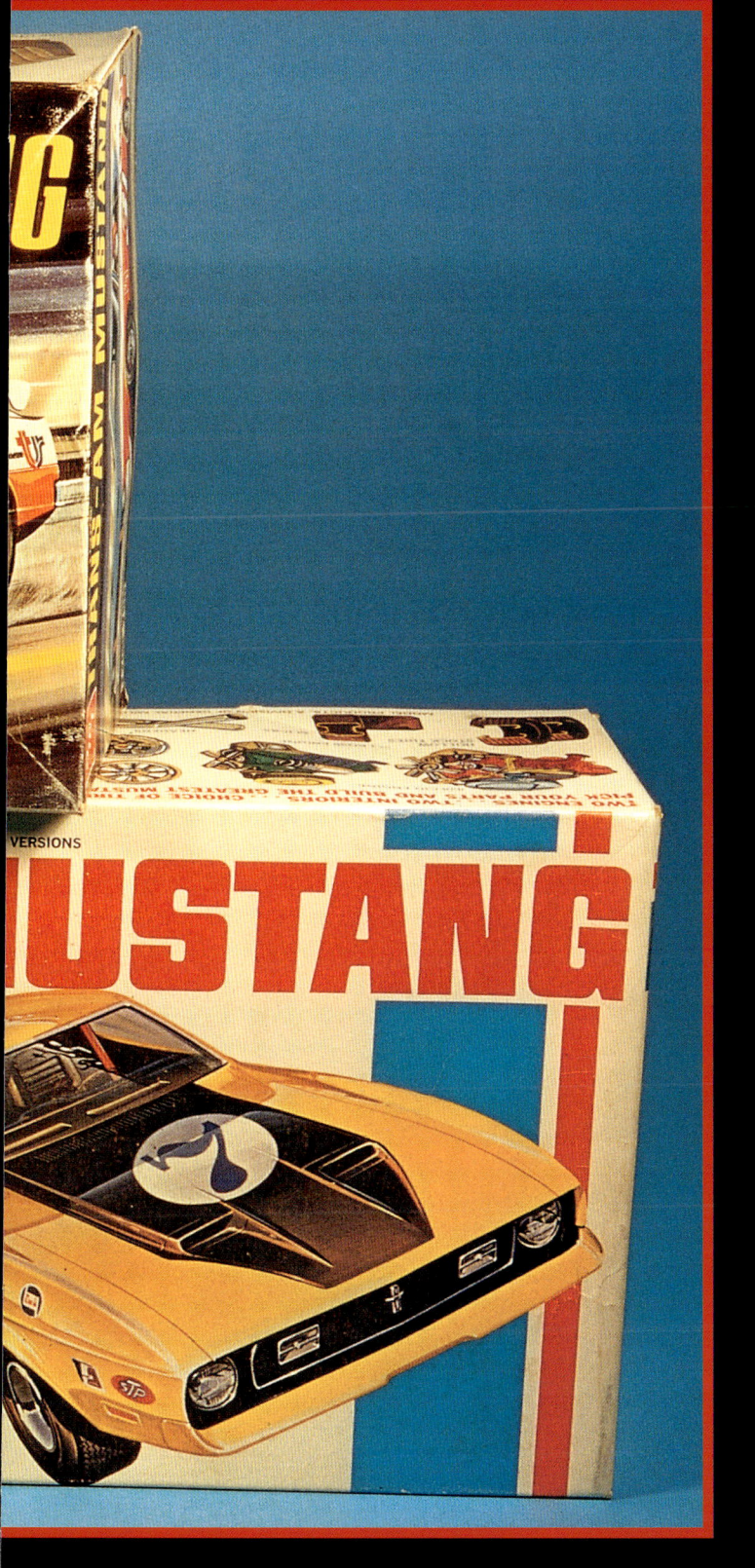

LAST OF GENERATION I, 1971–1973

The Ford Mustang for 1971 had a whole new look and feel. The new car was unmistakably a Mustang, but it was larger, heavier, and set no new design or engineering benchmarks. What started out in 1964 as a small, lightweight sporty car matured into a rather hefty boulevard cruiser. The wheelbase was increased an inch, and the width and length were increased a couple of inches. Large-displacement V-8 models had increased some 600 pounds in weight. A few new 1971 Mustangs weighed in at over 1.5 tons.

There were still an amazing 10 engine options for the 1971 Mustang—everything from an inline overhead valve (OHV) six-cylinder to the 429 Cobra Jet R. The Boss 429 was a distant memory, as was the Boss 302 for the new 'Stang. The 1971 Boss 351 came into its own as it benefited from the factory preparations for continued Trans-Am competition that never happened.

Here's a threesome of Generation I Mustang 1/25th scale plastic model kits. At top center is an original annual AMT 1973 Trans-Am Mustang kit No. 7206 with parts to build a road-racing version. At right is an original annual 1972 Mustang Mach I from MPC. At left is a 1973 AMT Mustang Mach 1 Street Machine kit No. PK-4167.

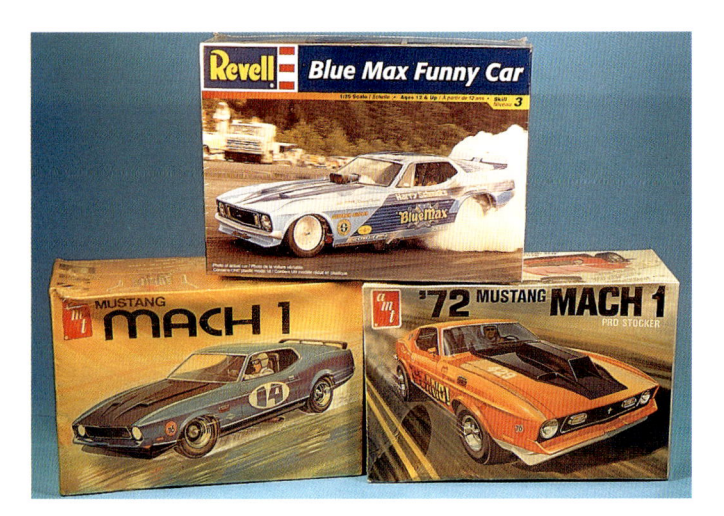

This trio of 1/25th scale, first-generation Ford Mustang plastic kits covers the spectrum from beginning to end. Top center is the Revell 1973 Blue Max F/C drag racer kit No. 85-7661 that was first issued in 2000. At left is an original annual AMT 1971 Mustang Mach I annual kit No. T-114 with extra parts and water-slide decals to build either a street-stock or road-racing version. At right is an original annual AMT 1972 Mach I kit No. T-335 with parts to build both production and drag racing versions.

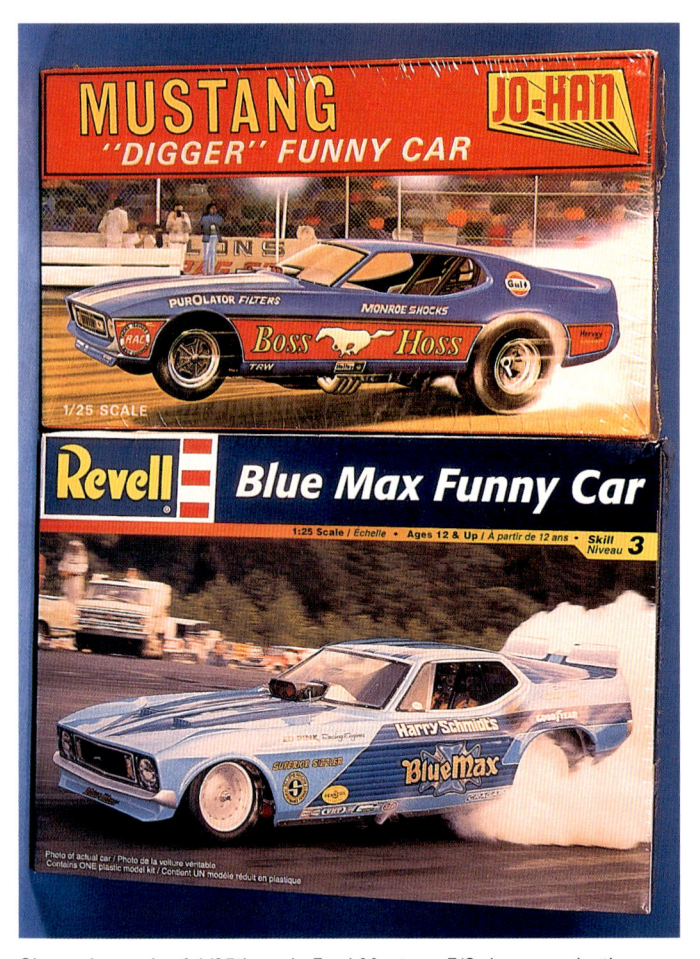

Shown is a pair of 1/25th scale Ford Mustang F/C drag car plastic model kits. At top is a JoHan 1973 kit No. GC 2100 that was last issued in 1985. At the bottom is a Revell version of the Blue Max Mustang F/C drag car kit No. 85-7661, first issued in 2000.

Three body styles—the coupe, convertible, and fastback—continued for 1971. The fresh exterior featured a larger, more aggressive Shelby Mustang–like grille treatment. The fastback, or SportsRoof as it was officially called, sloped to the rear end just shy of a 15-degree angle reminiscent of Ford's GT40.

Mustang sales, which had been on the decline since a peak of over 600,000 units in 1966, continued their downturn. Once more, the combined sales of Camaro and Firebird (167,754) barely topped Mustang for 1971.

Some Mustang competitors began to bail out of the pony car market as AMC ceased production of their two-seater AMX at the end of the 1970 model run. The AMX name would become the top-of-the-line model for the 1971-1974 Javelins. Just as AMC was exiting, the Dodge division of Chrysler Corporation debuted the Challenger as a serious contender to Mustang.

For 1972, sales did not improve. Mustang sales figures dropped again by nearly 25,000 units. The combined Camaro and Firebird sales also took a big hit and dropped to only 98,607 cars produced. Mustang had temporarily regained the top rank in the pony car market segment in sales, but no one at Ford celebrated.

Externally, the 1972 Mustang was virtually identical to 1971. The only real way to tell a 1971 from a 1972 was the style and placement of the Mustang script on the right rear of the car. There were fewer driveline options on the 1972 Mustang, but there was a wider variety of exterior and interior color choices for 1972, as well as snazzy seat and door panel fabric combinations and colors.

In 1973, the final year of Generation I production, Mustang sales were up slightly from the previous year, but the GM siblings' combined sales shot up to 143,064 to top Mustang sales by a few thousand cars. It was obvious the pony car market was dying off and in need of either a major overhaul, or complete and forced abandonment by manufacturers.

Mustang Production Figures
1971: 149,678
1972: 125,093
1973: 134,867

Motorsports Mustang I

Since Ford previously had officially withdrawn from all major-league motorsports, racing activities for the final three years of Generation I Mustangs were mostly non-existent. Bud Moore took his small-block V-8 technology, Grabber Orange paint, and the number 15 and headed back to the NASCAR Grand National circuit for battle. Many other competitors,

These five diecast Mustangs in two different scales are a few rare examples of this last body style of Generation I. At the back from the left: Corgi James Bond *Diamonds Are Forever* 1972 Mustang; a Corgi Mach I 1972 Mustang; and a Johnny Lightning 1972 Mustang Mach I from their Magna series. All three models look suspiciously like they are from the same basic tooling. At front from the left is an Ertl 1/64th scale 1973 Mustang fastback and a Johnny Lightning 1/64th scale Mach I.

when left high and dry by the Ford no-racing decision, sought an alliance with other manufacturers. Mickey Thompson struck a deal with Pontiac and drove a Grand Am–bodied Funny Car in NHRA drag racing to replace his Mustangs. George Follmer and Mark Donohue continued to compete in SCCA Trans-Am racing in AMC Javelins in 1971 with great success. AMC was the last remaining manufacturer to provide direct factory support in motorsports at the time.

Things were about to take a surprising turn for 1974. The seeds were already sown for some makes to disappear from the pony car market forever. Other pony cars would be revised in ways that were extremely controversial, yet highly successful. Some manufacturers would motor on and leave their existing product lines virtually unchanged. Insurance rates, environmental issues, and energy costs impacted economic issues to change things in this market segment forever.

Mustang I Collectibles

The final three years of Generation I Mustangs have only recently started to become popular with full-size Mustang collectors and enthusiasts. Dealer sales literature, promos and annual plastic kits are highly collectible. There have been a few diecast pieces and toys produced from this era.

Knowledge = Dollars + Sense!

If you are unfamiliar with the subject of collecting Mustang automotive memorabilia, learning as much about the types of things you want to collect is common sense and sound advice that goes a long way to make this pastime thoroughly enjoyable. Knowledge is the key element in making wise choices, purchases, swaps, or trades. Where do you acquire this knowledge? "Attend shows, talk to fellow collectors and memorabilia dealers, or go to auctions. Observe prices at swap meets especially when transactions are taking place," emphasized Mustang owner and collector Paul McLaughlin. Simply avail yourself to as many resources as time permits.

Another suggestion is to join a Mustang owners club because Mustang owners (and owner wannabes) collect memorabilia. It's a great place to exercise all the elements of this equation with a support group of others with similar interests. Learn and profit from their experiences, good and bad. Another valuable resource is the Internet. Visit Mustang-related chat boards and Web sites. Use a good search engine to browse the net for Web pages by individuals, manufacturers, or mail-order retailers.

Although your collection shouldn't necessarily be viewed as a business venture, sound judgment and minding your financial practices will certainly

Shown in their respective blister pack, is this pair of early 1970s 1/64th scale diecast Mustangs. At left is the Johnny Lightning *Diamonds Are Forever* 1972 Mustang. At right is the standard 1973 Mach I Mustang by the same company, Polar Lights.

The Japanese toy manufacturer Taiyo produced this tinplate version of a Generation I Mustang in 1973 and 1974. The piece is approximately 9-1/2 inches long, is battery powered with steerable front wheels, and has forward and reverse motion.

pay big dividends in the short term, and the long haul as well. It is, after all, a financial investment that could eventually be substantial. If price is not an object, then without any reservation I can assure you there will be hordes of willing takers for your cold, hard-earned cash! Be patient, cautious and, at times, a bit shrewd and you will be rewarded with a steady growth and cultivation of your collection in an orderly and efficient manner.

But, let's not forget to include the excitement of finding that one piece you've always desired. Personally, the joy is all in the anticipation of finding that special item. What makes the anticipation and acquisition even sweeter is adding it to your Mustang collection at a great price. After all, collecting and collections are really fulfilling a fantasy and appreciating each collectible as a small, but vital, piece of the Mustang legacy.

Since the storied introduction of the Ford Mustang nearly 40 years ago, thousands of collectible items have surfaced and are shown in this book. Some of these items remain plentiful today if you know where to look. That's where the increased awareness and knowledge comes into play. By comparison, some other pony paraphernalia was never produced in large numbers from the outset. These items were not designed to be "collectible." They were produced to meet a perceived demand and make a profit. "Many [items] are valuable today because thousands were most often played with and discarded. Very few survived in mint condition," emphasizes collector Wayne Moyer. "But today, hundreds of thousands of affluent 'big boys' would like to revisit their childhood experiences."

If you are new to this topic or are looking to become an active collector, it is time for stark reality to set in. That reality is positive even with a modest collection. A small collection already has value. In contrast, acquiring many older pieces will most likely be expensive. If this is your initial venture into Mustang collectibles, let's hope you are willing to settle for currently produced much less expensive Ford Mustang items. Otherwise, you will certainly need a substantial and steady flow of money for your hobby.

This "Gulper" Mustang Funny Car was produced by Matchbox and was part of their Speed Kings series in 1972.

AMT produced these annual 1/25th scale plastic 1971 and 1972 Ford Mustang promotional models for car dealers. These vehicles have remained very popular with collectors since they were issued.

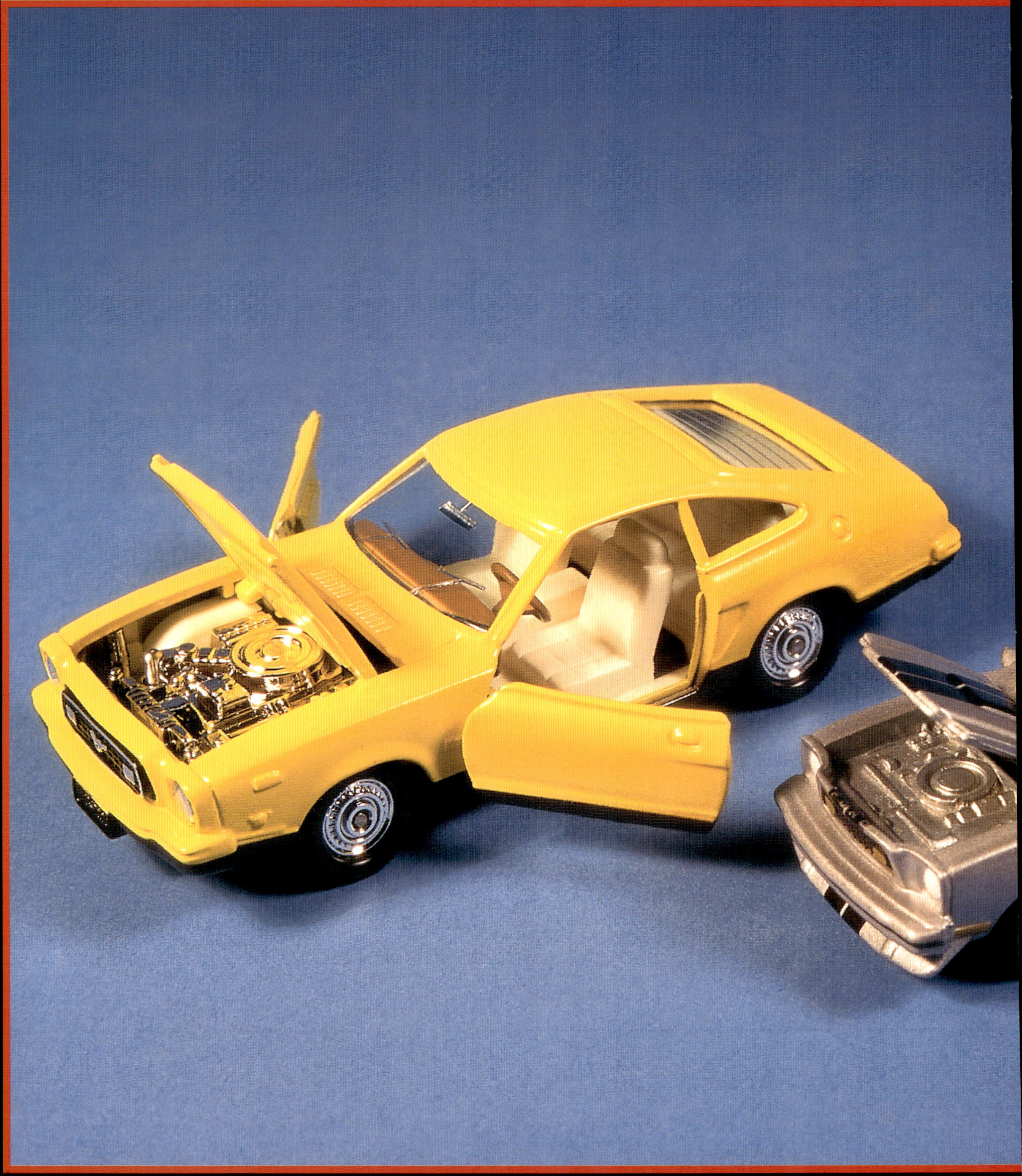

CHAPTER SIX

SECOND GENERATION, MUSTANG II, 1974–1978

As early as 1970, many people, including Lee Iacocca, knew something major had to change with the Ford Mustang. The once lithe and nimble pony had quickly evolved into a large and lumbering boulevard cruiser in less than a decade. By the close of the 1973 model year, Mustang production had fallen from a record high of 680,989 units at the end of 1965 to just 134,867 units for 1973. Drastic measures were needed.

Combined sales of GM's siblings, Chevrolet Camaro and Pontiac Firebird, continued at a steady pace and occasionally exceeded Mustang annual sales figures. The question of survival for the entire market segment for all manufacturers also was in question.

By 1971, Lee Iacocca had replaced Bunkie Knudsen as president of Ford Motor Company. Iacocca, in his new position at the top, was not about

---

There is little selection in 1/43rd scale diecast with the exception of this 1974 Mustang II fastback from Japanese manufacturer WEM. Polar Lights' Johnny Lightning diecast line of 1/64th models includes this well-done 1977 Cobra II. Note that both replicas feature opening panels like the articulated hood on the JL example. The WEM model's hood and both doors open, but the trunk lid is molded as part of the body shell.

Shown are the two original AMT 1/25th scale plastic promotional models of the 1974 Mustang II, which were only offered in two colors.

to see his greatest career accomplishment become an historic anomaly. Ford's new president wanted a "reinvented" Mustang similar to the first edition. Ford designers and engineers proceeded at a fever pitch to accomplish this task by the 1974 model introduction in the fall of 1973.

The final exterior styling for the new Mustang utilized a number of established marque design cues. The aggressive grille treatment, long-hood/short-deck silhouette, and three-element taillight treatment still identified the new model unmistakably as Mustang. Engineering dynamics based on modified production parts and assemblies, reduced curb weight, and smaller dimensions (including a shorter wheelbase of less than 100 inches) appeared to have the reborn Generation II Mustang headed in the proper direction.

Without question, the 1974 Ford Mustang II was greeted by the media and car-buying public with great enthusiasm. *Motor Trend* magazine saw fit to name the new pony as its Car-of-the-Year recipient. Siting the new era of conservation and environmental concerns, the *MT* staff presented the award stating, "simply put, it (Mustang II) is the right size at the right time for the greatest number of motorists."

Mustang II was nearly a foot shorter than the 1973 model. The wheelbase shrank from 109 inches in 1973 to slightly more than 96 inches for 1974. The curb weight in 1974 was nearly 500 pounds less than the 1973 version. There were no big displacement performance engines available for Mustang II, just a 2.3-liter inline four-banger and a 2.8-liter V-6.

Although Mustang II sold a whopping 385,993 units in 1974, the sporty car-performance enthusiasts were seriously turned off by the new generation of Mustangs. Many of these folks found solace in a Datsun (now Nissan) Z car, Camaro Z28, or a 6.6-liter Pontiac Firebird Trans Am.

Sales figures steadily declined over the next five model years of the Mustang II. Although this iteration of the original pony car was to be known as Lee Iacocca's "little jewel," the inclusion of a V-8 and even the introduction of special models, such as the Cobra II and King Cobra, never allowed the car to meet with favor among the hard-core Mustang faithful.

Mustang II Production Figures
1974:   385,993
1975:   188,575
1976:   187,567
1977:   153,173
1978:   192,410

Combined Camaro and Firebird Production Figures
1974:   224,737
1975:   229,833
1976:   293,734
1977:   374,588
1978:   459,915

Motorsports Mustang II

Through the five-year run of the Mustang II, there was little activity in motorsports. Legendary names such as "Dyno" Don Nicholson, Bob Glidden, and Shirley Muldowney carried the Blue Oval torch through the dark days of the mid-1970s. Glidden propelled his small-block Mustang II to the NHRA Pro-Stock title in 1975. Nicholson followed suit by taking the Pro-Stock title in the NHRA in 1977 and in the IHRA series at the wheel of a small-block Mustang II drag car.

In road-racing circles, independent competitor Charlie Kemp shocked the International Motor

MPC produced these two annual promotional models of the 1975 Mustang II for use through Ford dealerships that year. They were only available in one body style and in two colors, as shown.

Shown is a pair of MPC 1/25th plastic scale model kits of Mustang IIs. At top is the MPC 1974 original annual kit No. 7413. At the bottom is an MPC offering for 1976 kit No. 1-0773, a replica of the Mustang Cobra II.

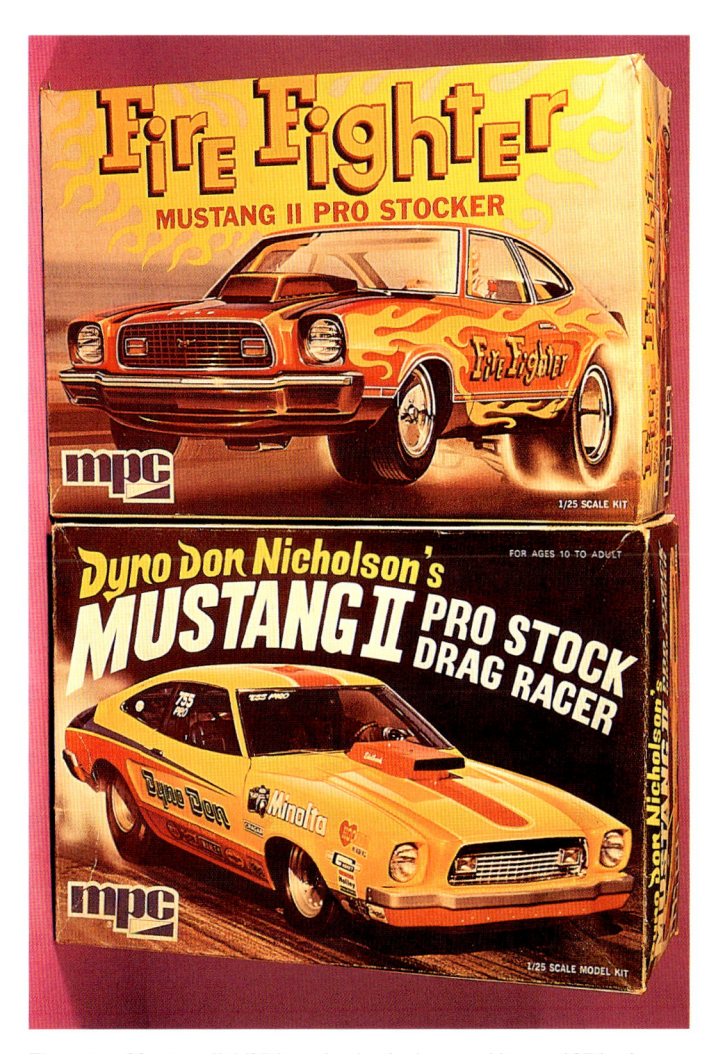

These two Mustang II 1/25th scale plastic drag car kits are 1974 releases from MPC. At top is a hypothetical P-S car kit No. 1761. At bottom is a replica of "Dyno" Don Nicholson's P-S drag car kit No. 1764.

Sports Association (IMSA) set with a one-off, full tube-frame creation he called *Kemp's Cobra II*. The purpose-built racecar, based on production sheet metal, was like nothing running in the series at the time. Describing this hand-built creation as radical would be using very modest terminology. Built by Kar Kraft with Jack Roush horsepower, the sanctioning body hassled Kemp wherever the car appeared for competition through the two-year season Kemp campaigned his Cobra II. The Kemp Cobra II is credited today with setting the standard for all grand touring (GT) prototype racecars that came after it.

Today, whatever feelings remain of the love/hate situation surrounding the original Mustang II, one thing transcends everything else. For most Mustang lovers, the II still doesn't warm their collective hearts, but one section of the car has found favor with the street rod and custom car set. Many such creations utilize Mustang II front suspension and disk brake assemblies.

Mustang II Collectibles

The Mustang II remains the least popular model among collectors. This is best reflected in the scarcity of Mustang II items. Due to this fact, there is a good selection of original factory dealer sales literature. Mustang II promotional models were done by AMT for 1974 and 1975. MPC and AMT produced 1/25th scale plastic model kits as both street-stock and racing versions.

Where to Find Collectibles

Sources for old or new Mustang collectibles are plentiful. A twist on an old adage might be, "Mustang collectibles are where you find them." Garage sales, toy stores, hobby shops, gift and specialty shops, swap meets, and local, regional, and national Mustang events are places to look. Frequently read the classified section of your local newspaper. Check the automotive categories, or look for categories with headings like "Memorabilia," "Automotive Collectibles," "Toys," "Model Cars," or "Sales Literature."

Although the box art looks quite similar, the two, 1/25th scale plastic model kits shown are actually different releases. On top is an AMT 1977 Mustang II kit No. 6560 that was issued in 1984. At bottom is AMT's 1977 Mustang II kit No. PK-4179, issued in 1982. The "PK" prefix in the product identification number indicates that it was issued during the brief period when Lesney (parent company of the Matchbox brand at the time) owned the AMT company.

These two, 1/24th scale plastic model kits are produced basically from the same tooling. At top is the Gunze-Sanyo kit of Charlie Kemp's Cobra II Sports Car Club of America (SCCA) racecar kit No. G-139-600, which was first issued in 1977. At bottom is a U.S. Airfix version of this kit, No. 8133.

Subscribe to collectibles newsletters, magazines, and periodicals that either cater specifically to the interests of Mustang enthusiasts or automotive memorabilia in general. Always be alert for the mention of special offers for Mustang collectibles in such diverse locations as in packaged food items, aftermarket automotive parts catalogs, or a special offer on the label of a household detergent container.

There are numerous retail sources for a wide variety of Mustang collectibles. Nearly all of these entities have a toll-free number, Web site, or an E-mail address for communicating with perspective customers. Some retailers primarily deal in older items while others can provide you with fresh product or selected, hard-to-find items that have increased in value over time. Some of the sources that advertising in print or online have an actual storefront location. Obviously, when a retail source is convenient to your location, frequent visits for browsing, gathering information, or purchasing is always the preferred choice. "Internet sites such as eBay.com facilitate millions of transactions each year. Choosing a category type from the main menu will allow you to browse through the listings being offered for sale," John Coulter said.

Without question, the best places to find the widest selection of Mustang collectibles firsthand are special single-make car shows and swap meets. Each fall, Lowe's Motor Speedway in Concord, North Carolina, plays host to the Grand National Mustang Show. Imagine a facility billed as the "Mustang Super Bowl" that literally overflows with every imaginable piece, part, toy, model kit, poster, dealer brochure, and more, in one spot at one time! Dealers and Mustang enthusiasts from literally all over the globe attend this annual event. With that level of participation, one is bound to find some irresistible "must-have" bargains.

Polar Lights has become a real competitor in the small diecast market with its Johnny Lightning 1/64th scale line. Shown are two of the Mustang II replicas from their Mustang Classics blister pack series. At left is a 1977 Cobra II, at right is an IMSA sports car prototype racecar Cobra II.

Ford Mustangs have always been popular outside of the United States. A good example is this 1976-1977 1/64th scale Mustang II from Argentina by the Jet de Gillette Company. This is car No. 9 from a set of 10.

An alternate choice would be the Performance Ford Club of America show held each year in Columbus, Ohio. Although it's an event for all Ford products, this expansive car show/swap meet is another primary source for the kind of eclectic collectibles on the radar scope of many Mustang aficionados. There are dozens of other Mustang/Ford meets all around the United States, plus some notable events in Germany, Great Britain, and Australia each year.

Once your collecting interests enter a more focused phase, there are special places to search and usually find what you're looking for. Plastic model kits, dealer promotional models, cast-metal and tinplate toys, and diecast models are among the hottest Mustang collectibles. Of course, newer items may be found in the usual places such as Wal-Mart, K-Mart, Meijers, Target, and Toys"R"Us. Most of the specialty magazines in this category feature display advertising from a wide variety of resellers that mostly carry new product, but some specialize in vintage Mustang models and toys from many eras. In most cases, you won't know what is available unless you ask. Even if there is no mention in a business advertisement about older Mustang items, you might be pleasantly surprised with what you discover.

MUSTANG
Motorcraft
QUALITY PARTS
Ford
ROUSH racing
GOODYEAR
Carlite
Jack Roush
BBS
Motorcraft
GT
Norelco

CHAPTER 7 SEVEN

GENERATION III —REBIRTH, 1979–1986

By July 1978, Lee Iacocca found himself out of a job just a few months before Henry Ford II was due to retire. At this same time, a totally new Mustang was on the way, and Ford Motor Company was setting all-time sales records.

Changes to the Mustang for 1979 were the most profound in the short history of this storied marque. Overall dimensions including width, length, and wheelbase grew a bit. Slightly more than 4 inches were added to the distance between the front and rear axles to provide more interior room, especially for rear-seat passengers.

Generation III's basic floor plan/chassis was a shared platform within the Ford family of unibody passenger cars. Initially developed as the underpinnings for the manufacturer's new intermediate line, Ford Fairmont and Mercury Zephyr, the platform was skillfully modified for use under the new pony. The "Fox" platform, as it came to be known, also saw service under the Thunderbird, Cougar, and Lincoln Mark VII through the 1988 model year.

Revell-Monogram's product manager Ed Sexton is a serious builder. Shown is a product of his handiwork based on Revell-Monogram kit No. 7155.

OFFICIAL PACE CAR
1979 INDIANAPOLIS "500"
PRODUCT INFORMATION

Here is an original 1979 Indy 500 pace car booklet. Measuring a standard size of 8 1/2 x 11 inches, this promotional piece came from Ford's Public Relations Department in late 1978. More than 30 pages of text feature numerous black-and-white photos throughout that depict the many modifications to the new Mustang as well as specifications and options used.

The Fox package for the 1979 Mustang was the first use of a modified McPherson strut front suspension system. Normally at the heart of this system's layout is a coil-over-shock-absorber-type cylinder (referred to as a strut). For this package, the strut was moved to the outside of the coil spring. The rack-and-pinion steering, first introduced to Mustang with the 1974 through 1978, was carried over to the new model. A solid, live, rear axle that was mounted to coil springs and a four-bar, trailing arms suspension was out back. This marked the first time Mustang did not ride on rear leaf springs.

Engine choices still included an OHV inline four, German-made V-6 that was replaced midyear 1979 by an OHV inline six-cylinder powerplant. A 302-cid V-8 was the top performance option for the third-generation 'Stang. However, even with a V-8, the 1979 Mustang was no hot rod because the 302 was equipped with just a two-barrel carburetor and a measly 140-horsepower rating.

Outward appearance is always the chief selling point for any car. The 1979 Mustang was no

Next to a full-size Mustang, this 1979 Pace Car go-cart is probably one of the largest pieces of pony car paraphernalia. Manufactured by the F.W. Company in Arizona, this limited-edition, motorized 'Stang (only 2,000 were produced) was sold for $695 as a promotional item through Ford dealers. *Ford Motor Company*

After years of the absence of any annual Mustang promotional models, Universal Marketing Company from Richmond, Michigan, produced this 1/25th scale Cobra model. This item didn't have the quality of earlier promotionals from AMT, and was not as readily available from Ford dealers. The author purchased this one via mail order; it was quite a struggle to get the order filled due to the rarity of the car. In spite of its availability, according to the *Autoquotes* promotional value guide by Butler and Young, this 1981 Cobra is relatively low priced.

exception in this respect. The external surfaces of the new pony shared nothing with previous years. The new Mustang had taken on a thoroughly European countenance. Gone was the trademark design which included the fish-mouth grille, concave side scoops, and three-element taillight treatment. These historic icon design features were replaced with a fresh, new silhouette available as a notch-back coupe or a semi-fastback hatchback body shell.

For the second time in Mustang's short production life, the 1979 Mustang was chosen to pace the 33-car field at the Indianapolis 500 Labor Day event. The actual car that paced the race was one of three pace cars made, and the handiwork of Cars and Concepts and Jack Roush Engineering. The trio featured a special T-top greenhouse and a potent race-worthy small-block V-8. Ford also created 11,000 street replicas readily identifiable by their special silver-and-black paint scheme that featured red and orange highlights. Replicas were manufactured with a pop-up sunroof, but the pace car graphics were a dealer-installed option.

To commemorate the 1979 Mustang Indy pace car, two companies produced models of this significant automobile. At top is the 1/25th scale MPC kit No. 1-0785; at bottom is the 1/24th scale Monogram kit No. 2250.

63

With the introduction of the Generation III Mustang in 1979, three different companies produced plastic scale model kits of the new pony. At top is the 1/25th scale MPC kit No. 1-0725, at left is the 1/24th scale Monogram kit No. 2260, and at right is the 1/25th scale Revell kit No. 7200.

Revell, Inc. produced this 1/25th scale plastic model car kit of the Mustang Motorcraft Turbo for release in 1979. This was a special promotional item for the full-size Ford Motorsports show car. There is no kit number on the box. The popular theory is that this kit was only available in California.

Many design elements from the 1979 pace car set the tone for future Mustang styling. The reardeck spoiler, front air dam, and rear-facing hood scoop became a regular part of the performance model appearance motif for the next few years.

Even though the Mustang was a totally new pony, sales for 1979 were only 369,936 units. At the same time, the GM siblings of Camaro and Firebird combined to sell just shy of 500,000 cars in the same year. Total sales in 1979 were nearly twice the number of cars sold the final year of the Mustang II.

Although the 1980 and 1981 Mustangs had the look of aggressive street marauders, as the saying goes, "beauty is only skin-deep." There were great-looking Cobra graphic packages on the three-door hatchback models, but performance actually got worse for 1980. The 302 V-8 for 1980 was actually reduced to 255 cid with a paltry horsepower output of only 119. To add insult to injury, this package was only available with an automatic transmission. For 1980, the combined sales of Camaro and Firebird were just shy of 260,000 units compared to Mustang's number of 271,322 for the same year.

Shown is a trio of early 1980s Mustang plastic model kits. At top is a Monogram Models 1983 1/24th scale LX convertible kit No. 2222. At left is an MPC 1/25th scale "Wild Breed" 1982 GT kit No. 1-0816, and at right is an MPC 1983 Mustang GT, 1/25th scale kit No. 1-0837.

By 1982, wiser heads were making final production decisions at the No. 2 automaker. The big news was the reintroduction of the Mustang GT as a serious performer. The 302 V-8 returned and was now called the 5.0 liter H.O. (for Height Output) with 175 horsepower. The revitalized GT was easily recognizable on the street with a new grille and hood scoop, and because it was only available in black, red, or silver.

In spite of a slight freshening of the grille and rear taillight treatment, the 1983 Mustang holds the unenviable position of being the lowest selling pony. Only 120,873 units were sold in 1983, and it became evident more "oomph" would be needed to once more elevate the Mustang to its premiere position in the marketplace.

For 1984, it first appeared that no action, or at least very little, would be aimed in Mustang's direction. The styling and mechanical features for 1984 were carryovers from the previous year. It wasn't until midyear that Ford showed genuine evidence that the "internal gears" were in motion. This corporate effort was better known as the Special

Tom Creeger built this superb example of the Monogram 1/24th scale plastic model kit No. 2222.

65

Shown is the plastic kit box and built model of Monogram Model's Miller Mustang in 1/24th scale kit No. 2296. This model put Monogram Model on the map among racecar model builders. The author built the finished model in the foreground.

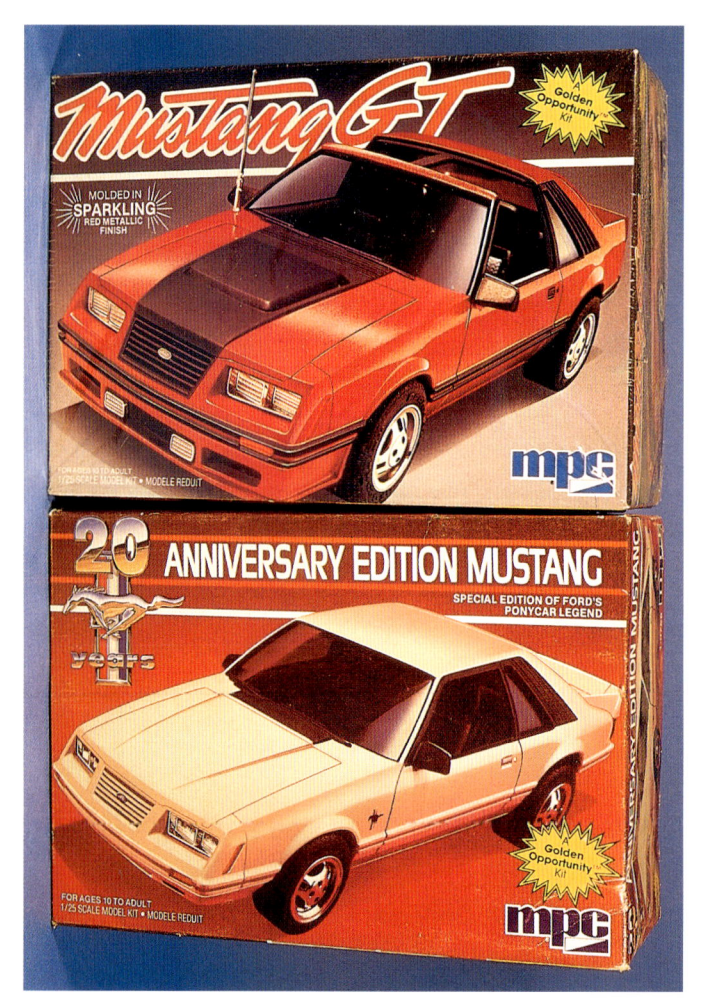

Here's a pair of 1/25th scale Mustang plastic model kits by MPC. At top is a 1984 GT kit No. 1-0877, and at bottom is kit No. 0768, a replica of the 20th anniversary GT350.

Vehicle Operation (SVO), which later became the Special Vehicle Team (SVT) in 1993. A special upscale performance Mustang was introduced midyear that broke the stalemate in not only appearance, but in drive train technology.

The Mustang SVO was unlike any other pony. The styling, which included an off-center functional hood scoop and by-plane rear-deck spoiler, made this Mustang a unique visual treat, but what really showed the results of thinking outside the lines was the power train. The SVO was powered by a 2.3-liter overhead camshaft (OHC) turbocharged inline four with a whopping 205 horsepower. That number was just five ponies shy of the mighty thundering 5.0-liter V-8. In a comparison test in a popular magazine at the time, the SVO ran virtual circles around a V-8-equipped Chevrolet Camaro. Unlike both the Mustang GT and General Motor siblings, SVO's strong suit was world-class handling as well as amazing throttle response.

Ford issued a special series of 20th Anniversary edition Mustang GT350s in 1984. These special ponies were available as hatchbacks or convertibles. The only color available was Oxford White with a Canyon Red interior and nostalgic rocker panel striping. Some pundits believe that Carroll Shelby wasn't too pleased with the unauthorized use of his copyrighted model designation, which resulted in the construction of only 5,260 units.

By 1986, the SVO was overpriced, and the four (even with its turbo clout) was not in the tradition of the raw-power, rumbling V-8-equipped Mustang. The SVO only lasted through the 1986 model year. However, it's influence in both styling and performance-enhancing features had a profound influence on all future Mustangs. Mustang styling for 1985-1986 again received a freshening and showed the SVO influence. The horsepower rating for the 302 was upped to 210. It all worked as planned, and sales were back up to nearly 225,000 units by 1986.

Mustang III Production Figures
1979:   369,936
1980:   271,322
1981:   182,552
1982:   130,418
1983:   120,873
1984:   141,480 (+ 5,260 20th anniversary GT350 editions)
1985:   156,514
1986:   224,410

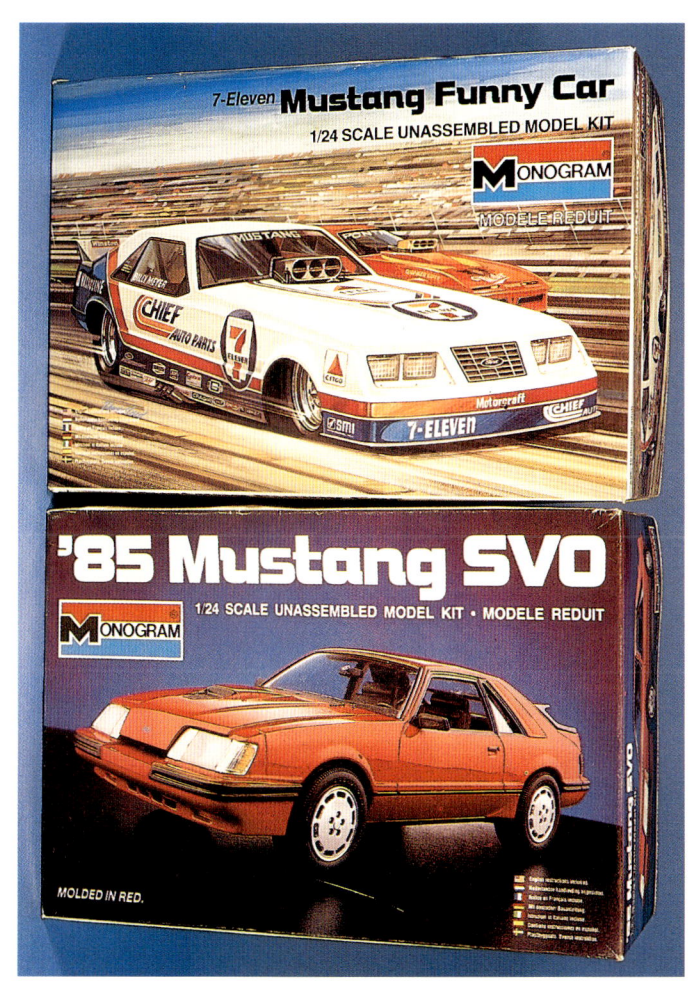

Shown is a pair of very special mid-1980s Mustangs in 1/24th scale plastic kits by Monogram Models. At top is a replica of the 1984 Billy Meyer 7/11 NHRA Funny Car drag car kit No. 2710. At bottom is a replica of the 1985 SVO Mustang kit No. 2243.

Tim Boyd built this excellent replica of Monogram Models' 1985 Mustang SVO from kit No. 2243.

Here's a trio of 1986 Roush Racing IMSA GTO road-racing Mustangs produced in 1/24th scale plastic kits by Revell. At top is the Folgers Mustang kit No. 7154, at left is the 7/11 Mustang kit No. 7153, and at right is the Motorcraft Mustang kit No. 7155.

Camaro and Firebird Production Figures

Year	Figures
1979:	494,025
1980:	259,345
1981:	197,038
1982:	116,362
1983:	229,265
1984:	389,895
1985:	275,898
1986:	302,682

Motorsports Mustang III

Ford returned to major-league motorsports in America in 1981 in an unusual fashion. If you're thinking NASCAR, Formula One, Indy cars, and Trans-Am, you couldn't be more wrong. Factory officials were intrigued by the successes of the Zakspeed Mercury Capri that had shown a great deal of strength on European road courses in the late 1970s. German racing ace Klaus Ludwig was the lead driver of these purpose-built Mercs.

Ford was persuaded to finance the construction of similar tube-frame rolling chassis of modified production 1981 Mustang sheet metal. Two cars were built by German racecar builder Erich Zakowski, the No. 6 Miller Mustang and a No. 16 Motorsports Mustang. In early events, the fleet ponies that were piloted by Ludwig and Indy car pilot Kevin Cogan gave fits to typically dominant foreign hardware including Porsches. Ludwig managed to finish second in his first outing in the car and won outright at Sears Point, California, a little later in the season. This victory had a strong influence on Ford's upper management's decision to return to major-league motorsports.

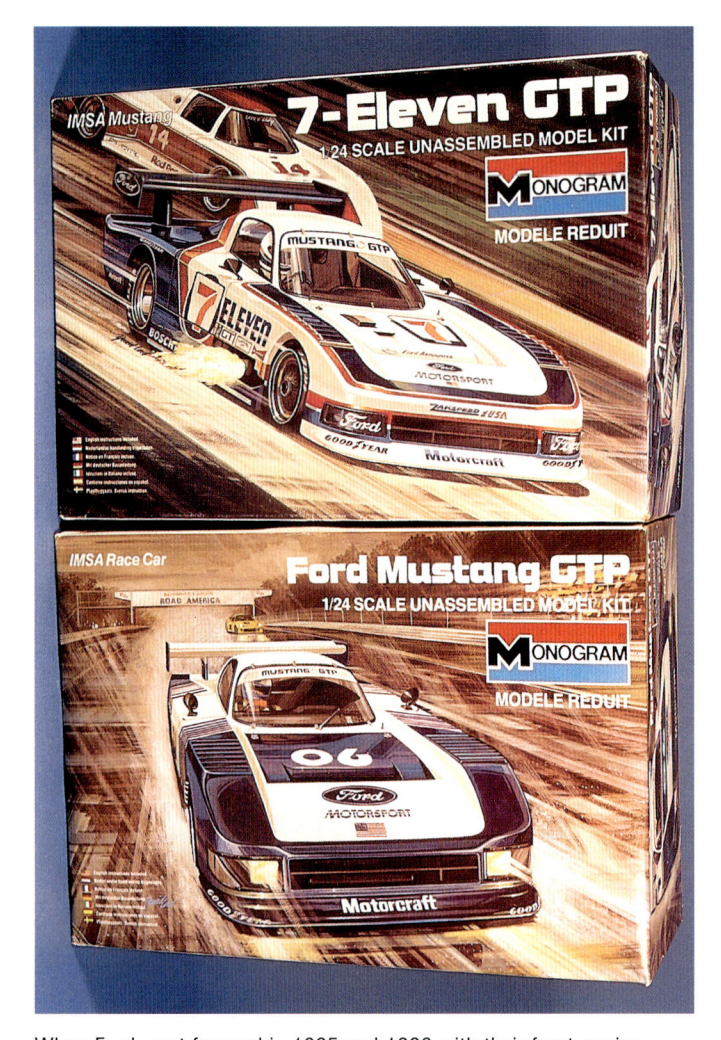

So far, this Georgia Marketing & Promotion's 1984 1/18th scale Mustang SVO is the lone example of diecast replicas of this notable mid-1980s turbocharged pony.

When Ford went forward in 1985 and 1986 with their front-engine Mustang GTP program, Monogram Models followed suit with these two 1/24th scale plastic model kits. At top is kit No. 2709, and at bottom is kit No. 2708.

The Italian company Burago produced this 1/24th scale Mustang Highway Patrol car in 1983 under the product No. 0185. The model includes a detailed interior in a basic gray color, with opening doors and a hood with engine compartment features.

In the SCCA professional Trans-Am road-racing series in 1981, Tom Gloy drove a Ford Mustang to victory. This was Ford's first major racing victory since it withdrew factory support in 1970.

In 1984, Jack Roush Engineering fielded purpose-built IMSA GTO (Grand Touring Over 2 liters) Mustang racecars and started a long and dominant association with the professional sports car series. That initial season saw Wally Dallenbach Jr. and Willy T. Ribbs outclass all competitors in the quest for the championship title.

Again in 1985, Dallenbach teamed with John Jones and Doc Bundy to win the GTO class during the 24 Hours of Daytona event. In 1986, Roush cars dominated in the twice-around-the-clock event. This time it was Scott Pruett and Olympian Bruce Jenner who topped the charts and captured the GTO class title.

Mustang III Collectibles

Original issue 1/25th scale plastic model kits are very sought-after collectibles of this generation. However, sales of such items began to decline and manufacturers quickly took note. The days of annual Mustang plastic kits were coming to an end. Oddly, model kits are worth far more not built, although examples done by well-known, established, or professional builders can bring high prices due to their quality and scarcity.

Annual promotional models are virtually non-existent during this period. Only a single example is documented here. After 1981, it would be another 13 years before such items would be manufactured once more.

Many original-issue diecast and plastic toys exist and are sought-after collectibles. Mustang replica cars of this era are growing in interest to full-size automobile collectors, and are appealing subjects for high-end manufacturers including Georgia Marketing & Promotions.

Determining Value

Once armed with information contained in the Price Guide in the back of the book, a quick conclusion is that even a modest collection may be worth hundreds or thousands of dollars. Dealer sales literature, plastic model kits or annual dealer promotionals, books, apparel, or some variety of assorted specialty items are obviously worth much more than you originally paid for them.

Most of the older annual Mustang promotional models and plastic model kits in pristine condition can command upwards of $100 to $200. Even recent releases of diecast models or toys—especially if they are limited production items—are beginning to rise in value due to the market. More often the price or value of any Mustang collectible listed in a published guide is generally based on like-new, original condition items.

For model kits, toys, and promo and diecast models this means sealed, cellophane-wrapped original packaging in excellent condition. For plastic model kits the universal rule of thumb has always been that once the seal is broken, the value plummets quickly. The only way the unwritten rule could be amended is if a particular item was so rare the buyer was willing to pay whatever it took to own the piece.

Although building a model kit normally diminishes its value, there are exceptions. Any model kit built by a recognized skilled craftsman may result in the finished piece being worth many dollars. Like a painting by a noted artisan that demands big bucks, a model built to professional or museum-quality standards is a highly prized collectible.

Eclectic items such as a can of Mustang beer, Mustang cigarettes, Mustang silk underwear, or a Mustang Avon bottle are all influenced by the same set of standards as other Mustang memorabilia, although pinning down a fair value is often much more difficult. According to collector Wayne Moyer, an item is worth exactly what someone will actually pay for it at the time product and money change hands.

Georgia Marketing & Promotions (GMP) is responsible for this jet-black 1/18th scale 1985 Mustang GT. This replica features opening panels, considerable chassis and engine compartment detail; virtually every bell and whistle is included in the interior.

Revell-Monogram's product manager Ed Sexton is a serious builder. This is a product of his handiwork based on the R-M kit No. 7155.

Ed Sexton, also built this Mustang GTP from his company's kit No. 2708. Note the level of detail on the miniature turbocharged, inline four-cylinder engine.

Revell
#25 Roush Raci
Model Kit/Modèle Réduit
MUSTANG
Ford
GOODYEAR
SCCA
TRW
EAGLE

CHAPTER EIGHT

A Fresh Face, 1987–1993

The exterior of the 1987 Mustang displayed a strong styling influence derived from the controversial SVO enthusiast model produced from 1984 through 1986. This was the first major body restyling since the Generation III was introduced in late 1978. The lower body was much more aerodynamic and featured softer, rounder lines and surfaces. By this point, virtually the entire Ford passenger car line had adopted the aero-look. Mustang was finally catching up with the other family members.

In 1987, for the first time, the LX and GT models were set apart with distinctly different front- and rear-end treatments. The LX line looked pretty much the same as before when viewed from the rear and in profile. However, the most notable changes were to the front fascia. Here the new nose featured a lower grille opening with a single horizontal bar emblazoned with a floating Blue Oval badge. The new look was topped off with wraparound, flush-mounted integrated turn signals/headlights.

Mike Madlinger built this replica of the 1989 championship winning No. 25 Roush T/A Mustang from kit No. 7195. The original kit box is shown in the background.

Shown is a pair of 1/25th scale kits from the same tooling by two different manufacturers, although Racing Champions/Ertl currently owns both the AMT and MPC lines. At top is the current reissue of the original 1988 MPC Mustang GT under the AMT name, kit No. 30272. At bottom is an example of the original issue of the MPC 1988 'Stang under its own name, kit No. 6211. After skipping a couple of years, this was the lone 1988 Mustang kit for a few years.

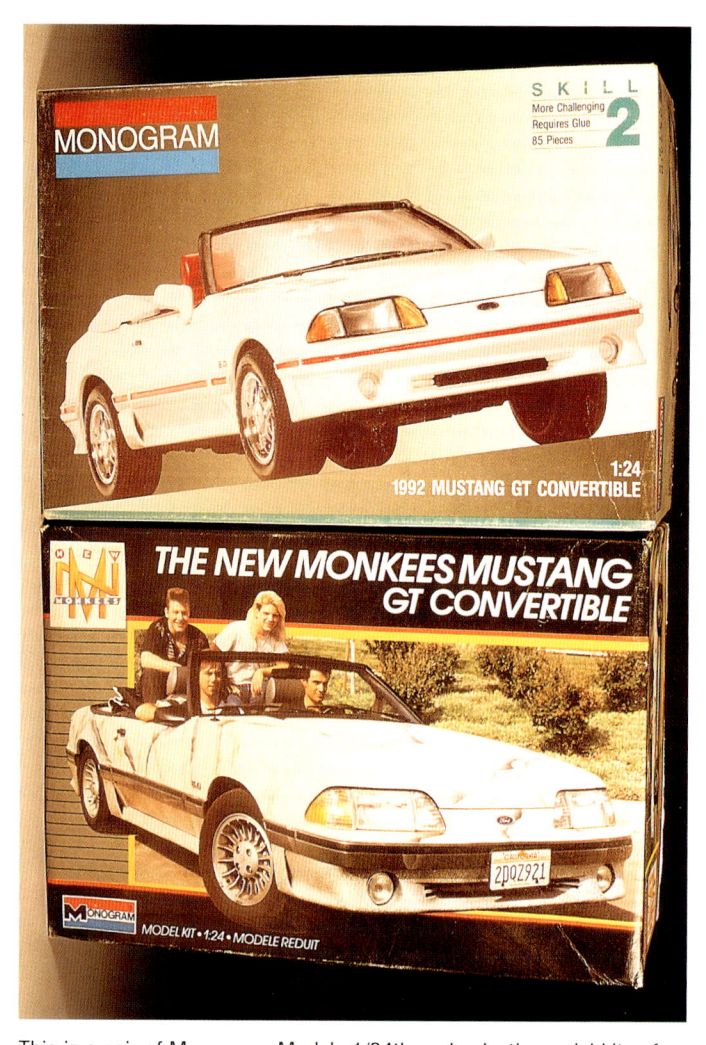

This is a pair of Monogram Models 1/24th scale plastic model kits of the late 1980s and early 1990s Mustang GTs. At top is a 1992 version of the ragtop pony kit No. 2953. At bottom is a 1988 kit No. 2771 version of the same car packaged in preparation for a revival of the Monkees television show with a new cast and set of wheels. The new program was a "no show." The kit is modeled with a strange swirl pattern in a light blue styrene plastic.

By contrast, the new GT looked quite different from any angle. The front end now had no upper (above the bumper) grille opening; only the Blue Oval badge centered on a clean body color panel between the same headlight combo used on the LX. Extensive body cladding was used for the 1987 GT where side skirts incorporated dummy air scoops aft of each wheel opening. The changes to the rear of the new GT were unmistakable and featured a distinctive louvered taillight panel.

Underneath, many of the SVO driveline and suspension refinements had finally found their way into the new GT. Bigger brakes, beefier suspension components, and turbine-style aluminum wheels were upgrades for the new GT.

For the next five years, Mustang remained a steady performer and was changed little, although minor upgrades continued to be made in optional trim, special exterior colors, and creature comforts.

For the final year of Generation III production (1993), Ford threw the virtual "kitchen sink" into the venerable pony car. Among the many enhancements for 1993 was the return of the legendary Cobra name, which many pundits and enthusiasts agreed was a major high mark for the marque.

The 1993 Ford Mustang Cobra was visibly different from the other models. A new grille opening up front, unique body side skirting, an exclusive reardeck spoiler, and low-profile 245/45ZR Goodyear Eagle tires mounted on special 17-inch alloy wheels made the new Cobra an attention grabber on any boulevard. The trusty 5.0 V-8 was warmed up to 235 horsepower with the use of GT40 free-flowing cylinder heads. Only 4,993 1993 Cobras were produced.

With the absence of available annual Mustang plastic model kit releases, companies like Revell continued to fill the gap with excellent racecar releases. Shown are three 1/24th scale plastic model kits of Roush road-racing Mustangs from the 1989 SCCA Trans-Am season. At top is the No. 25 car that Jack Roush specifically hired Dorsey Schroeder to drive (kit No. 7195). At left is the Whistler Mustang that was occasionally driven by Schroeder (kit No. 7197). At right is the JPS car driven by Finnish driver Robert Lappalainen (kit No. 7196).

There were also 107 very special 1993 R model Cobras produced by Ford's SVT operation. These stark white "snakes" were meant for all-out competition, and were stripped of all amenities because they were intended to be serious club racers.

Mustang sales continued to be sporadic for 1987 and 1993. The sole show room competition continued to come from GM's sibling pony cars, the Camaro and Firebird. Their yearly combined sales figures often outsold Mustang.

Mustang Production Figures
1987: 159,145
1988: 211,225
1989: 209,769
1990: 128,189
1991: 98,737
1992: 79,280
1993: 114,228

The first SVT Mustang Cobra was offered for sale by Ford in 1993. This 1/24th scale Revell-Monogram plastic model kit No. 2530 is the only example in miniature of this significant 'Stang to date.

Shown is a hand-built 1/43rd scale model of the Roush Mustang Tom Kendall drove to the 1993 IMSA championship title. There were fewer than 350 kits manufactured for Ultimodels in California. Floridian Peter Wingfield built approximately 100 examples, including the one shown.

This is a pair of 1/43rd scale diecast 1993 Mustangs that competed in the German Touring Car (DTM) Series in 1993 and 1994. Both models were manufactured by Minichamps and are extremely difficult to find in the United States.

SVT Cobra Production Figures
1993:   5,100 (includes 107 Rs)

Camaro and Firebird Production Figures
1987:   226,373
1988:   158,731
1989:   175,254
1990:   55,501
1991:   135,148
1992:   98,279
1993:   53,867

Motorsports Mustang

During the Generation III period, Jack Roush Mustangs continued to dominate in major road-racing series including the IMSA GTO and SCCA Trans-Am. The Roush juggernaut also continued to crush the competition in world-class events like the 24 Hours of Daytona and the 12 Hours of Sebring.

In drag racing, Ricky Smith won the 1987 AHRA Pro-Stock title in dominating fashion by winning 11 of the series events. Unlike the NHRA where P-S engine displacement is restricted to 500 cid, Smith's Mustang was equipped with a 700-

Georgia Marketing & Promotions recently produced this 1/18th scale replica of a 1986 Mustang LX Georgia Interstate Highway Patrol car. This replica features opening body panels, a correct law enforcement interior, a high-output 5.0 V-8 under the hood, and a detailed trunk including appropriate firearms.

plus-cid V-8 engine derived from the old Boss 429, commonly referred to as a "mountain motor."

Also in 1987, Steve Saleen Motorsports Mustangs won the SCCA SS/GT title. Winning drivers on the Saleen team included owner Steve Saleen, Rick Titus (son of late and legendary Jerry Titus), and Pete Halsmer.

The Ford Mustang juggernaut continued to dominate big-time in the late 1980s. Jack Roush hired Dorsey Schroeder to drive the lead car in a multi-car onslaught to win the 1989 Trans-Am title for Ford. It was the Mustang's 25th anniversary, and the driver and manufacturer's championships were perfect presents. Schroeder delivered the goods, and won the driver and manufacturer's titles on his way to the championship.

Tom Kendall charted new territory in the record books when he went to work for Jack Roush. In 1993, Kendall walked off with the championship title in the IMSA GTO series. Kendall's streak would continue with the SCCA when he established many enduring records in the storied Trans-Am road-racing series.

Mustang Collectibles

The most desirable Mustang collectibles continue to include annual dealer sales brochures, plastic scale model kits, diecast cars, and to a lesser degree, various toys. These types of collectibles stay at the top of the list for 1987 through 1993, especially for the years where there were special production models or highly visible and successful Mustang racing vehicles. Originally, there was a sprinkling of diecast cars and toys for this period. However, annual model kits and dealer promotional models fell on hard times. It was only in later years, (the late 1990s to early 2000s) that this era spawned a much wider assortment of three-dimensional collectible items. There remain many significant 1987-1993 Mustangs that have received little attention.

Building Plastic Kits and Collecting Promos

Plastic scale models, both factory-assembled and unassembled kits, became popular in the late

This collection of late 1980s and early 1990s Mustang models in different scales provides a variety of what is available for this era. Included is this GMP 1/18th scale Trans-Am Mustang driven by 1989 champion Dorsey Schroeder during the 1990 season. From left: a 1/43rd scale diecast 1990 GT convertible by New-Ray, a conversion of the Ertl 1989 convertible to resemble Wayne Moyer's car, and an original Ertl 1/43rd scale diecast. In the foreground is a pair of built resin kits assembled by Wayne Moyer. At left is a 1/43rd scale Secret Mustang driven by Lynn St. James from the French company Starter. At right is a Pro-Line 1/43rd scale resin kit of the General Chemical Mustang that was driven in the 1992 IMSA GTO series by Ford executive Mike Dingman.

1940s and early 1950s at about the same time plastic was discovered as a useful by-product of petroleum distillation. Promotional models were originally developed for new car dealers to enable them to provide potential customers a more precise idea of what the new full-size vehicles looked like. In the mid-1950s, boxing up an unassembled promotional model and calling it a kit proved to be quite popular with consumers. This was the rudimentary beginning of the plastic model kit business. By 1958, the original Aluminum Model Toy (AMT) Corporation perfected an approach to utilize a method where common tooling was used to make both assembled and unassembled products. The unassembled item differed from the promo in that polystyrene plastic was used in making the model kit.

The whole promo and kit collecting frenzy reached a fever pitch at about the same time the Ford Mustang was conceived and eventually manufactured in the early 1960s. At first, AMT had the whole Mustang market to itself. At the time, AMT was first headquartered in Troy, Michigan, conveniently close to the heart of the American auto industry in Detroit. AMT is credited with establishing the preference for 1/25th scale in the United States when they manufactured the first promotional models and unassembled kits in this scale. With 1/25th scale, each inch on the model represents 25 inches on the full-size subject. Although the rest of the world's

Show and concept cars have been an integral element in the Mustang lineage for nearly 40 years. Shown are three examples of the 1993-era Mach III show car developed by Ford's styling department to forecast design cues for the next-generation Mustang. Included is the 1/18th scale version from Jouef, a 1/43rd scale replica also from Jouef, and a 1/64th Super Wheel version by Motor Max.

model builders and collectors prefer 1/43rd or 1/24th scale, we Americans have always preferred 1/25th scale.

Building plastic model Mustang kits is a whole separate issue. The age-old debate has been whether one should build a vintage unassembled kit, or leave it in original, unassembled pristine condition. The fact is that building a model kit most often results in the decreased value of that model. Some collectors are horrified to find that a builder has desecrated a valuable collectible. Others remind us of the overriding purpose for all plastic model kits. After all, they were produced to be built.

In most cases, the value of a vintage unassembled plastic model kit drops by 75 percent once it's built, but this idea is debatable. My advice to all collectors and builders is simple: Unless you have above-average model building skills, leave the precious—not to mention very expensive—parts and pieces in the kit box. Or, do what works best for you.

A controversy also exists with diecast collecting. Collectors of diecast models will pay a high price for unrestored models with visible signs of wear. The debate is, "to restore or not." In many other branches of the collecting hobby, complete restorations are commonplace. Farm tractor and implement collectors spend huge amounts of money to get older pieces restored. Be advised that restoring an older Mustang diecast to like-new condition will impress some collectors and infuriate others.

The first SVT Mustang Cobra was offered for sale by Ford in 1993. This 1/24th scale Revell-Monogram plastic model kit No. 2530 is the only scale model example of this significant 'Stang to date. Paul Grala built this replica and used factory-correct Teal Metallic automotive paint.

AGES 4 AND UP
WINNER'S CIRCLE
HIGH PERFORMANCE
DIE CAST COLLECTIBLES
WARNING:
CHOKING HAZARD-Small parts.
Not for children under 3 years.
Castrol GTX
SUPERMAN
Asst. No. 55500
ohn Force
ETIME SERIES
NO. 7 OF 8
JOHN FORCE
Castrol GTX

CHAPTER NINE

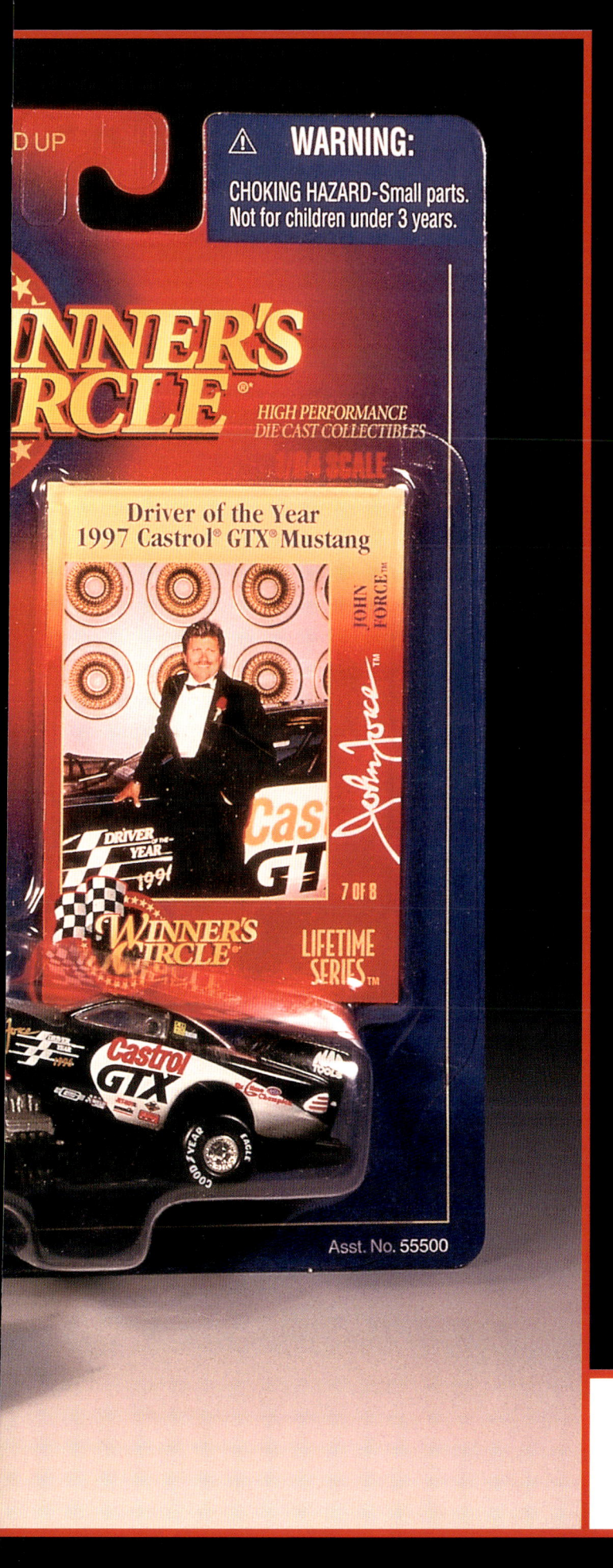

GENERATION IV, 1994–1998

The details of the fourth-generation Mustang were still up-in-the-air as early as the mid-1980s. The trusty Fox platform–based version had served the marque quite well from its inception with the 1979 model year and was basically unchanged through 1993.

Gradually declining sales along with a desire to revamp the Mustang led corporate planners, designers, and engineers to consider more than one direction for the new car. One concept that received serious consideration really shook things up. It would have been a totally new type of Mustang based on a Mazda front-wheel-drive platform. Actually, the new car was a re-skinned Mazda MX-6 sports coupe. The sheet metal, nameplate, and scripting would have been the only Mustang elements, and the remainder of the car was all Mazda with none of the "fixture features" identified with this segment icon. This vehicle was eventually manufactured as the Ford Probe.

Hasbro's Winner's Circle series offers 1/64th scale diecast models of many of the important Mustang racecars driven by John Force. Included here are replicas of the 1999 Superman, 1998 Elvis, and 1997 Driver of the Year Mustang Funny Cars that were driven to fame and fortune by the flamboyant Force.

Ertl/AMT was still in the dealer promotional business in the mid-1990s. Shown is a pair of 1994 Mustang GT 1/25th scale promos issued by the Dyersville, Iowa, company under a licensing agreement with Ford.

When word leaked out in the mid-1980s about what Ford might have in store for the legendary pony car, the dyed-in-the wool Mustang loyalist would have none of it. Thousands of angry letters flooded into the world's second largest car maker. Let's just say the general tone of the letters was gritty, and each writer got quickly to the point.

In the fall of 1988, the decision was made to develop a new Mustang in the mold of the original concept. That meant a front engine, V-8, and rear-wheel drive that utilized as many of the accepted engineering and visual design elements as possible. A small proprietary development team was assembled that included engineers, industrial designers, product development, and marketing personnel that included Mustang Program Manager Ken Dabrowski and Engineering Program Manager John Coletti. This effort also benefited from the inclusion of many former SVO alumni. The new hush-hush operation was housed out of sight and away from the main factory facilities.

The plan was to create a fresh new Mustang that incorporated many previous popular design elements. The Fox platform was so thoroughly reworked that although it had some passing resemblance to the original, it was considered to be new. However, since its heritage was obvious, it was dubbed "Fox-4." The exterior design was much softer and rounded than previous Fox-based Mustangs. The new grille treatment, side scoops, and tri-lens taillights spoke volumes about the lineage of this pony. By mid-1990 the looks and mechanicals were pretty much established. The launch of "Job One" (beginning actual production) was December 1993.

The SVT Cobra concept had started with the 1993 model year, and was carried over to the new generation Mustang. This special version was again called Cobra, and set higher standards for the marque. The new Generation IV Mustangs set a new benchmark for the market segment. The SVT Cobras from 1994 through 1998 featured the best of everything including suspension, brakes, wheels, a hand-assembled double overhead cam V-8 that put out more than 300 horsepower, and a 460-watt sound system.

Visually, Mustang changed very little between 1994 and 1998, and mechanically, there were some major changes. The year 1995 marked the final time the Mustang was equipped with the push-rod 5.0 V-8. This trusty powerplant would be replaced in 1996 by a version of the corporate modular 4.6-liter (260 cid) V-8 engine.

Ford's SVT group built 250 R model Mustangs strictly for show room stock racing events. These nearly hand-built vehicles used the larger 351-cid push-rod V-8 that pumped out 300 eager horses. The potent engine was backed up by a competition-proven Tremac five-speed transmission. The R model was stripped of most creature comforts and the Special Vehicle Team added in the best brakes, suspension, and BFGoodrich 45ZR-17 tires on all four corners.

Beginning in 1996, Mustang received a new modular engine and an improved Borg-Warner T-45 five-speed transmission. Externally, Mustang had a new three-element vertical taillight treatment very similar to the original 1965-1966 Mustangs. Otherwise, the original Generation IV Mustang motored on pretty much unchanged through the 1998 model year.

Ertl/AMT produced this pair of Generation IV Mustangs in 1/25th scale plastic model kits. The Snapfast Plus Mustang GT rudimentary kit No. 96-8118 is at the top, and at the bottom is a SVT Cobra glue kit No. 97-8231.

Shown is a trio of 1/25th scale Ford Mustang dealer promotional models. Clockwise from left: 1996 Moonlight Blue, 1994 Laser Red, and 1995 Arctic White.

81

These mid-1990s Mustang plastic scale model kits are all from Revell. The Super Stallion (SS) kit No. 2571 (left) was a late 1990s show car that debuted at the North American International Auto Show in Detroit, Michigan. The SS proved cars could be both awesome performers and environmentally clean. The Mustang Mach III (middle) was an early 1990s show car that forecasted design cues for the Generation IV Mustang kit No. 7364. The Boss Mustang (right) was a limited-production, high-performance Cobra designed by the late Larry Shinoda (kit No. 6390).

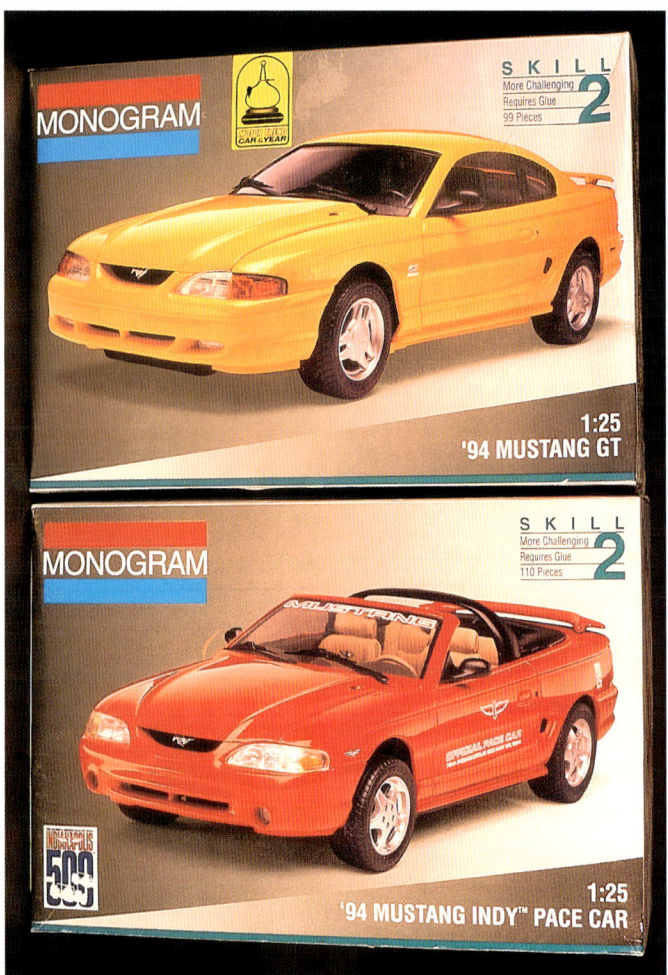

Mustang IV Production Figures
1994:   137,074 (includes 6,009 SVT Cobras)
1995:   185,986 (includes 5,258 SVT Cobras)
1996:   135,620 (includes 10,006 SVT Cobras)
1997:   108,344 (includes 10,049 SVT Cobras)
1998:   175,522 (includes 8,654 SVT Cobras)

Camaro and Firebird Production Figures
1994:   161,574
1995:   180,910
1996:   97,764
1997:   126,566
1998:   109,355

Motorsports Mustang IV

The Generation IV Mustang was selected as the pace car for the 1994 Indianapolis 500. This was the third time the marque paced the 33 starters in the Labor Day classic. Ford used their new SVT Cobra convertible. The hot performance model remained pretty much unchanged from production status except for speedway-mandated safety features such as a fuel cell, roll bar, fire suppression system, and

This pair of plastic model kits is by Monogram Models. Both items represent 1994 Mustangs. At top is a kit of the *Motor Trend* Car of the Year kit No. 2967. At bottom is a replica of the 1994 SVT Cobra Indy 500 pace car kit No. 2975.

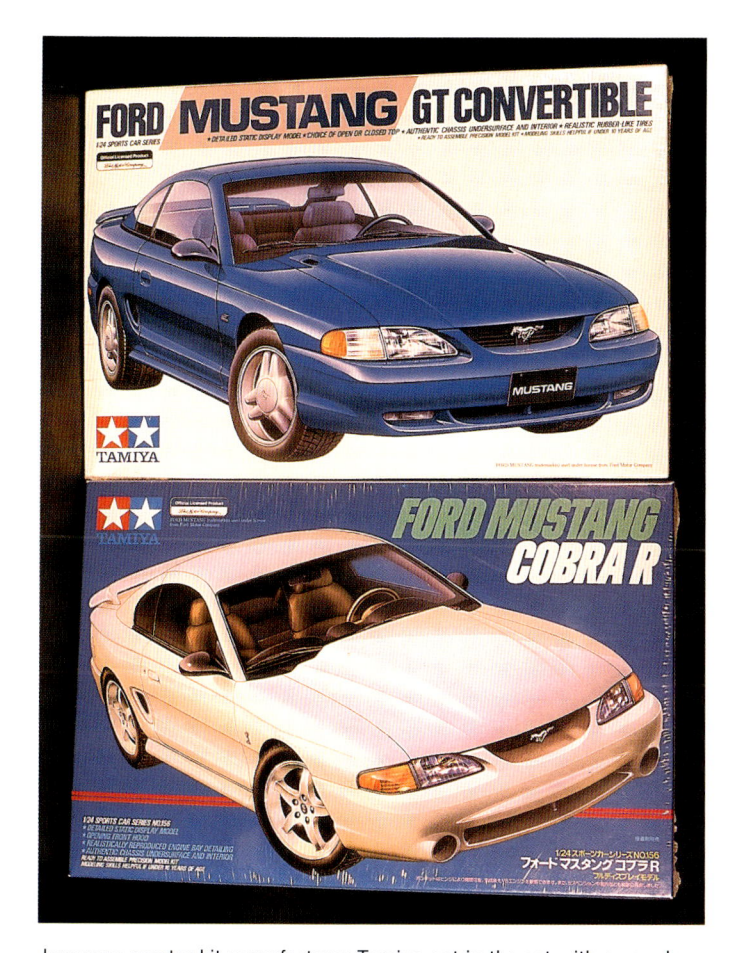

Japanese master kit manufacturer Tamiya got in the act with a couple of its 1/24th scale Mustang kits, after the introduction of Generation IV in 1994. At top is a GT convertible that could be built with a detachable top (kit No 24141). At bottom is the only kit of the 1994 SVT Cobra R model kit No. 24156-1800.

strobe lights. The standard five-speed transmission was replaced with a four-speed automatic.

A run of 1,000 replicas was built and offered for sale to the public through the normal channel of SVT Ford dealers. Parnelli Jones, the winner of the 1963 Indy 500, drove the pace car during the event.

After Tommy Kendall won the Trans-Am title for Chevrolet in 1991 and secured the IMSA GTO title for Roush Racing, he moved on to the SCCA Trans-Am series. From 1995 through 1997, Kendall once again totally ruled the series. T.K. not only won three consecutive championship titles in the series, but he broke Mark Donohue's long-standing record of eight consecutive victories and won 11 wins in a row out of 12 races during the 1997 season.

On his 70th birthday, renowned racer and Academy Award–winning actor Paul Newman drove the *Nobody's Fool* Mustang, sponsored by the movie of the same name, to the class title at the 1995, 24 Hours of Daytona. Newman remains the oldest person to ever win a major motorsports event, and he did so in a Ford Mustang.

In drag racing, Ford Motor Company moved quickly to fill the void that was created by the sudden retirement of driver Bob Gildden, their most noted motorsports celebrity. For 25 years, this legendary Pro-Stock racer recorded an NHRA record of 85 event victories and 10 championships. Superstar John Force was lured away from GM and rolled out his lightning-fast Funny Cars with new Mustang

Shown is a pair of hand-built, cast-resin 1/43rd scale models of two Roush T/A Mustangs that were driven to series titles by four-time champ Tommy Kendall, and built by Peter Wingfield. The All Sports 1996-1997 version is on the left, and the 1995 version is on the right. Both models were built from photo-etched and cast-resin parts produced by Pro-Line Racing Miniatures. There were probably less than 100 built models and 250 kits produced of either car.

83

On his 70th birthday, renowned racer and Academy Award–winning actor Paul Newman drove the *Nobody's Fool*–sponsored Mustang to the class title at the 1995, 24 Hours of Daytona. The Oscar-nominated Newman starred in the film, *Nobody's Fool.* Newman remains the oldest person to ever win a major motorsports event, and he did it in a Ford Mustang. This 1/43rd scale model was built from photo-etched and cast-resin parts. There were approximately 250 kits made of this model by Pro-Line Racing Miniatures and less than 100 built versions were produced. This model was built by Peter Wingfield.

This quartet of diecast Mustang convertibles represents the best of the top-down ponies from the late 1990s. In the background is a Jouef 1/18th scale 1994 SVT Cobra Indy pace car; in the center is a pair of Maisto 1/24th scale Mustangs, at left is a 1998 Cobra, at right is a 1998 GT; and in the foreground is a 1/43rd scale 1998 GT by New-Ray Toy Company.

84

Auto Art is recognized for top-quality 1/18th scale diecast models. Here is its 1998 Saleen Speedster S351 coupe in a screaming yellow color. The model literally has all the "bells and whistles," including a full-detailed interior, engine compartment, and well-defined chassis and suspension details. The Auto Art Performance Saleens set a new mark for 1/18th scale diecast models. The fit and finish is second to none, and the attention to detail is simply mouth watering to a true Mustang model lover. Every aspect of these unique machines has been captured from the finish that looks to be an inch deep, to the intricately detailed supercharged V-8 engine, to the wheel, tire, and visible vented four-wheel disk brakes with Alcon four-piston calipers.

fiberglass body shells. Force immediately cashed in on the new deal with Ford and won his seventh national championship title in 1997. He also captured the crown every year in the 1990s except for 1992.

In 1998, Force became the first Funny Car driver to set a new speed record in the quarter mile—faster than a Top Fuel dragster! Since Force came to the Blue Oval he has not been beaten, winning five straight NHRA Funny Car titles in a row. Moreover, He is the only 11-time national champion in this professional straight-line sport.

Aftermarket Ponies

Aftermarket tuners and specialty constructors including Saleen Motorsports, Keith Brown, Roush Industries, and Steeda tweaked already potent ponies into some of the most awesome street performers in the history of the marque. The Saleen S251 and S351 models possess the looks and performance of which legends are made.

Steve Saleen has emerged as the "Carroll Shelby" of the new millennium. There are a number of "tuner

This Auto Art 1998 Saleen Speedster S351 convertible is an exact replica of the famous aftermarket Mustang manufacturer pony products. In 1/18th scale, this diecast model is well appointed with exceptional interior, engine compartment, and chassis details. Auto Art Performance Saleen Mustangs are recognized as the standard for high-quality 1/18th scale diecast models. The fit and finish, and attention to detail simply make these scale replicas a must-have for the true Mustang model collector.

Renowned drag racing champion John Force scored many of his 11 NHRA Funny Car titles at the wheel of a purpose-built racing Ford Mustang. This Action Performance 1/24th scale 1997 Motorsports Driver of the Year diecast Castrol Mustang model replicates the car Force raced during the U.S. Nationals at Indianapolis Raceway Park in 1997.

This is a 1/24th scale Action Performance 1997 John Force Mustang Funny Car that features the standard Castrol paint scheme. When Force was aligned with Ford Mustang, together they "lit the rocket" that led to John's five titles in a row.

car" builders—specialists who bring their considerable engineering expertise to a vehicle. But, Saleen is one of the few specialty vehicle manufacturers to move the existing good looks of the Mustang to another level. His S351 models in coupe and roadster body styles provide the Mustang with an enhanced appearance and the performance to match the eye-popping styling.

Much like Carroll Shelby in the mid-1960s, Saleen not only builds his version of the Mustang, but he has raced them both domestically and overseas in such events as the 24 hours of LeMans and Daytona. After 16 years and over 7,000 vehicles produced, Saleen's cars have a reputation for performance that surpasses many of the world's most expensive and exclusive makes.

Mustang IV Collectibles

Established trends in the market remain unchanged as the most desirable Mustang collectibles continue to include annual dealer sales brochures, plastic scale model kits, diecast cars, and to a lesser degree, various toys. Sales literature for the SVT Cobra is already bringing high prices, especially for the years where there were special production models or highly visible and successful Mustang racing vehicles.

Manufacturers such as Mattel, Matchbox, AMT, Revell-Monogram, Maisto, Auto Art, and Minichamps remained active in the scale replica marketplace. Through these companies' efforts, a wide selection of diecast, plastic model car kits, and toys were produced for this period. For the first time since 1981, annual Mustang dealer promotional models were produced by AMT in 1994, 1995, and 1996. However, the assortment of annual model kits began to decline, and subsequently, Mustang dealer promotional models have not been produced.

Action Performance has an exclusive contract to replicate John Force Mustangs in scale diecast form. Shown is a pair of very collectible Force ponies. The special Elvis paint scheme, used at Memphis, Tennessee, in 1998, was the result of a sponsorship arrangement with the organization that represents the business interests of the late performer and Graceland. It didn't hurt one bit, as John Force is a *big* Elvis fan! At right is the special gold paint scheme used at selected events in 1998 to commemorate Force's seven Funny Car titles. Live on the QVC channel, Force used a chain saw to cut up the fiberglass body shell of the real car to auction off the pieces to lucky callers.

This quartet of diecast Mustang convertibles represent the best of top-down ponies from the late 1990s. In the background is a Jouef 1/18th-scale 1994 SVT Cobra Indy pace car. In the center is a pair of Maisto 1/24th-scale Mustangs, on the left is a 1998 Cobras, and on the right is a 1998 GT. In the foreground is a 1/43rd-cale GT by New-Ray Toy Company.

Revell Complete — It's all you need!

'99 Mustang Cobra

1:25 Scale / Échelle • Ages 10 & Up / À partir de 10 ans • Skill 2

WARNING: PLASTIC GLUE COULD CATCH ON FIRE. IT COULD HURT YOU IF IT GETS ON YOUR SKIN OR IN YOUR EYES. CONTAINS: METHYL ETHYL KETONE. Read Warning on Side Flap.

AVERTISSEMENT: LA COLLE À PLASTIQUE PEUT S'ENFLAMMER. SON CONTACT SUR LA PEAU OU DANS LES YEUX PEUT S'AVÉRER DANGEREUSE. CONTIENT DE LA MÉTHYLETHYLCETONE. Lire l'avertissement sur le rabat extérieur.

Mustang Cobra

CHAPTER TEN

THE EDGE LOOK, 1999 AND BEYOND

In 1999, only five years into the Generation IV Mustang, Ford designers applied a controversial surface treatment to the lower portion of the Mustang's body shell that is usually referred to as a "face lift." The "edge" look featured noticeably sharp-edged convex creases or break lines as part of the surfaces of the sweeping exterior curves. This actual aesthetic discipline was applied to the new-production Mercury Cougar and the 1999 Mustang that was introduced in the fall of 1998. Someone in the domestic automotive press at the time described the startlingly unique look of the Mustang exterior as, "a baseball cap sitting atop a shoebox." The lower body had taken on a decidedly angular look, but the designers had retained the soft, rounded top surface as a carryover from the Generation IV Mustang exterior. Controversial or not, the new look was popular as indicated by the production figures.

This Revell-Monogram 1/24th scale plastic model car kit No. 85-2151 is one of the few examples of items of the current generation of Mustangs. This is from their Complete kit line No. 85-2151. This kit contains a paintbrush, three bottles of enamel paints, and a tube of model cement, and is primarily aimed at younger builders.

There's not much choice in plastic scale model kits to pick from for the 1999 and later Mustangs. Shown are two variations of a 1/24th scale 1999 SVT Cobra plastic kit produced by Revell-Monogram. At top is the regular glue-style kit No. 85-2525, and at bottom is a Complete-style kit No. 85-2151 from the same Revell-Monogram tooling. This kit contains a paintbrush, an assortment of three colors of bottle-style enamel paints, and a tube of model cement.

The year 1999 marked the 35th anniversary of the Mustang, and Ford produced a special model to commemorate the feat. The 35th anniversary treatment was applied only to the GT model. Along with special black body and hood trim, the commemorative GT received unique 17-inch wheels, badges on the front fenders, and a special black-on-silver interior.

The new SVT Mustang Cobra received an independent rear suspension (IRS) for 1999 that improved handling and reduced the car's weight by 125 pounds. The 281-cid quad-cam V-8 supposedly got another 15 horsepower to up the horsepower ante to an advertised 320. Rumors were spread that the 1999 Cobra engine was down on power, and some owners had their cars dynoed. The rumors turned out to be true, and Ford recalled the unsold cars and remedied the problem for the cars that had been sold with engine and exhaust system upgrades. There were no SVT Cobras offered for sale to the public in 2000, but the top pony was again offered for sale in 2001.

A special run of R model Mustangs intended for serious competition was produced by Ford SVT. The prototype 2000 R had its first public outing at the National Mustang Convention at Lowe's Motor Speedway in Charlotte, North Carolina, on April 17, 1999. With its menacing and aggressive exterior, which included a revised nose and bulged hood

Three manufacturers of small, 1/64th scale diecast produced these models of the 1999 Ford Mustang. From left: Johnny Lightning's 1999 Mustang GT convertible from its Modern Muscle series; Matchbox offers this 1999 Mustang hardtop in its Mattel Wheels series; and the Hot Wheels 1999 Mustang coupe from the Mattel Wheels series.

Johnny Lightning produced this pair of Trans-Am 1/64th scale Mustang diecast models as part of its Muscle Machines series in 1999. At left is the Preformed Line Products pony that was driven by Randy Ruhlman. At right is the Homelink 'Stang that was driven by Paul Gentilozzi to the T/A championship in 1999.

treatment, 18-inch wheels, and reardeck horizontal wing, the 385-horsepower juggernaut was the fastest, and best performance Mustang ever. The prototype was painted in 1969 Mustang Calypso Red to give the new model a retro connection to the past. The 2000 R models were painted Performance Red, which is just a shade or two from the Vibrant Red used on the first SVT 1993 Cobra.

In spite of a few technical glitches and some controversy over its styling, Mustang continued to cream the competition through the 2001 model year. Rumors began to circulate that the only remaining domestic competition from GM, the Camaro and Firebird, was on the ropes and might be dropped from production. In the fall of 2001, General Motors announced the 2002 model year would mark the end of both the Chevrolet Camaro and the Pontiac Firebird.

Mustang started the whole pony car phenomenon in the spring of 1964, and for 2003, Mustang will become the only domestic survivor of this once rowdy, diverse, and well-populated market segment. A few rumors have slipped out from inside the Blue Oval fortress to suggest that the next-generation Mustang has now been rescheduled for the 2005 model year. Maybe the company is going by the old adage, "If it ain't broke, don't fix it!"

Mustang Production Figures
1999:   133,637
2000:   215,393
2001:   155,162 (includes 5,582 *Bullitt* models and 7,251 SVT Cobras)

Camaro and Firebird Production Figures
1999:   74,576
2000:   73,144
2001:   61,196

Shown is a pair of Maisto 1/24th scale diecast Mustangs. At left is a 2000 SVT Cobra coupe, and at right is a 1999 GT convertible. These two samples were purchased at Wal-Mart.

Motorsports Mustang

Mustang continued to be at the forefront in road racing in 1999. Veteran racer Paul Gentilozzi, who switched from Corvette to Mustang during the 1998 season, drove the Rocketsports/Homelink Trans-Am Mustang to the series title in 1999 and recorded seven victories in the process. It was a head-to-head battle with fellow Mustang driver Brian Simo, but on the season's homestretch, Gentilozzi prevailed.

In the professional ranks of drag racing, John Force continued on his relentless quest of rewriting the record books by winning NHRA Funny Car titles in 1999, 2000, and 2001. At the close of the 2001 season, Force was stuck on 98 event career victories, and surpassed Bob Glidden's former record of 85 in 2000. The string of 11 F/C championships is a record not likely to be eclipsed or equaled anytime soon. Force remains unbeaten in the NHRA's premier full-bodied, straight-line series championships since he joined Ford in 1997.

Mustang Collectibles

Traditionally, dealer sales literature, promotional models, and annual plastic model car kits have led the way with collectors. It's way too soon to forecast

Maisto and Polar Lights produced these three 1999 Mustang diecast models. From left: the JL 1/64th scale 1999 Mustang convertible; the Maisto 1999 Mustang convertible in 1/43rd scale, and the 1/24th scale 1999 GT convertible. These items were widely distributed and available in retail and discount toy and hobby stores.

Shown is a pair of Action Performance 1/24th scale diecast models of John Force's Funny Car Mustang racecars. In the background is the special Superman paint treatment that Force used to win the inaugural Top Fuel versus Funny Car invitational event at Bristol, Tennessee, in 1999. It was part of a special promotion that was used by champions in racing, including NASCAR, Indy cars, and sprint cars. John Force has had such phenomenal success in drag racing that his cars often have special paint schemes at many events each season. In the foreground is the special nine-time champion paint scheme Force used on his car in the final event of 2000.

The 1999 model year marked the first major styling change to the reborn Mustang that was introduced in 1994. For many it was a "love or hate" situation. The soft, gently flowing curves of the 1994-1998 body shell were replaced with decidedly angular shapes, or "edge styling," according to Ford. For some, the dramatic departure from the earlier look put their teeth on "edge."

Love it or hate it, the new Mustang is very distinctive, and not easily mistaken for the earlier years. The new car must be striking a chord with many people as sales of the controversial pony are on the increase again.

The 35th anniversary for the legendary pony car was in 1999. To commemorate the landmark occasion, Ford released an anniversary edition of the Mustang available in a restricted number of colors. Like the white sample shown, the special exterior treatment included a revised grille mesh, a unique hood scoop and rear deck spoiler, and 17-inch alloy wheels. Production was limited to just 5,000 units.

Maisto has created a small herd of 1999 Mustangs including two convertibles (in red and black), three coupes (in green, yellow, and silver), and a 35th anniversary coupe (in white). Fit, finish, and attention to detail are excellent. The Maisto folks have again upped the ante by equipping their new Mustangs with working coil spring suspension on all four corners. The beauty of this feature is that it not only works, but Maisto was able to achieve the proper ride height for their Mustang.

how annual dealer sales literature for 1999 and beyond will appreciate in value. Special issue pieces, like those for the SVT Mustang, have always been highly valued by collectors. There's no reason to think this trend will not continue.

There have been no annual promotional models produced for the years 1999 to the present. The last such item was the 1/25th scale 1996 Mustang promo by Ertl/AMT. There will likely not be any new Mustang promotional model until Generation V arrives in 2005.

Revell-Monogram is the sole manufacturer to produce a plastic scale model kit of a 1999 Mustang. This particular kit was offered in two different packaging versions. Since the time of this 1999 release, there have been no other plastic scale model kits produced. There is also a lack of post-2000 diecast and toys. There have been diecast models produced by at least four manufacturers of 1999–2000 Mustangs in prices ranging from under $1 to near $75, and in a range in scales from 1/64 to 1/18. There is a profound absence of Mustang paraphernalia for this period (1999 to present).

Mustang Product Licensing

A major factor that governs virtually every aspect of manufacturing any product associated with a patented or copyrighted image in the marketplace today is licensing. Defined as "the legal permission to engage in some business activity," licensing can best be described as obtaining legal authorization to use the signature, name, or likeness of a person, corporate symbol, product logo, or the exterior shape of some automobiles.

Because virtually everything in business is viewed as a revenue source today, personal signatures, a person's image, and even the three-dimensional shape of certain automobiles carries a legal registered copyright these days. Licensing has quickly become a steady flow of revenue generated by and through granting exclusive rights of registered trademark commodities for business purposes.

Licensing allows manufacturers of Mustang collectibles to legally produce a specific product or a line of products. Since licensing is such big business today, small, medium, and large corporations now

Shown is a pair of Action Performance 1/24th scale diecast models of two John Force Mustangs. In the background is the paint scheme from the final national event of the 2001 season. In the foreground is the special Universal Pictures Monsters promotion paint scheme with a likeness of Frankenstein that was used on Force's racecar in 1999. This particular scheme was used around Halloween.

have entire departments, or at least a qualified staff professional, solely dedicated to governing the entire process from original concept to retail store shelves. Not too many years ago, producing such products was not strictly regulated, and often the auto manufacturers considered products that included a wide variety of products such as plastic kits, toys, key fobs, neckties, and diecast models as free advertising.

The licensing fee charged by the grantor is eventually folded into the final retail price to the ultimate consumer. This fee may be a one-time lump sum and can be a rather large amount paid up front. It's more likely to be a combination of an up-front charge with a percentage paid on each item produced. A notable amount of the retail price of a plastic kit, diecast model, or a toy Mustang can be traced to the cost to obtain legal licensing.

A few years ago, American automakers began regulating these aftermarket products in an attempt to protect their intellectual property. Coincidentally, this action came along at about the same time they lost a substantial market share to foreign competitors. Although this can't be substantiated, the whole affair continues to generate millions of dollars for corporate coffers.

There are reportedly some benefits to the consumer as a direct result of the more recent, stricter licensing procedures. Among these benefits is the reasoning that close scrutiny, from concept through the manufacturing activities of the licensee by the grantor, will assure an accurate and quality product at a reasonable price. What has been found to be more realistic is a simple fact, "You only get what you pay for." Usually with the higher the price of an item, the better the attention to detail and overall manufacturing quality. This is especially important for scale model kits and diecast cars. This axiom doesn't always ring true since there are dozens of inexpensive Mustang products of high quality and accuracy on the market today.

Product licensing is now a fixture and will be with us for many years to come. Although these procedures do increase costs, they may also make the cost of doing business so expensive it will restrict a few manufacturers from participating in the marketplace.

Storing, Displaying, and Transporting Collectibles

When those few irresistible Mustang knicknack items you have brought home grow to a number that demands attention, you need to consider cleaning, storage, and display options. Here are some suggestions to help you take care of your collection.

Much too often valuable collectibles have been permanently soiled or heavily damaged due to improper storage. You can't expect dealer sales literature, postcards, posters, and other collectible Mustang paper products to survive unscathed in dirty or humid environments such as a basement, garage, or trunk of the family sedan. A clean, dry, corrugated shipping box is a good beginning storage container. Flat items, such as brochures, need to be wrapped in a plastic sleeve or inserted into large sealed plastic bags. Proper storage in plastic also keeps out moisture, dust, dirt, and pesky varmints or insects.

If you aren't ready to display your collectibles, leave them properly wrapped, packed, and protected. This allows for safe storage, and it is an ideal and practical solution if your Mustang collectibles need to survive. Three-dimensional items such as plastic kits, diecast models, and various toys require just as much attention as paper products because most of these items can suffer from the ravages of too much time in cold, damp, dark places. "I use plastic storage bins that slide easily under a bed or couch. The bins are protective, virtually dust free, and keep your valuable items away from little fingers…if you have kids," says collector John Coulter. Without taking some measures to protect your collectibles, they can easily fall prey to adventurous, inquisitive, and destructive two- and four-legged perpetrators.

Displaying your Mustang collectibles requires a definite commitment and some planning for the best results. If your personal stash includes a large array of product types, it will necessitate more creativity than if it's primarily of one category.

Displaying three-dimensional items including plastic promos, diecast models, or various types of toys may be the easiest to present. Individual clear plastic cases by companies such as JoHan, AMT, or Revell-Monogram can be found in major retail chains, hobby shops, or purchased directly from mail-order sources. Most of these cases feature an opaque base with a clear, lift-off, five-sided top. Some cases interlock and are stackable to allow you

Action Performance has an exclusive contract with John Force to replicate his Funny Car Mustangs in 1/24th diecast form. This paint scheme racecar has the most extensive level of detail of any such factory-built model available at the time this book was published. The original packaging is often quite colorful and makes a striking display with the diecast model, as shown here. Your Mustang diecast model will always have more value if it has the original packaging.

to safely display individual items, and maintain each collectible in a near dust-free environment. "Never, ever place any display case where direct sunlight shines on your valuable collectibles. Constant exposure is very destructive to many things, virtually bleaching out the color or actually melting some materials," emphasizes Wayne Moyer.

Maybe you desire something more elaborate to allow the luxury of "mixing and matching" product types. A factory-built display case with adjustable shelves, lights, and plenty of exterior glass panels is the ticket. These display cases are available in small wall-mounted units, or medium sized and larger floor units, and can be Spartan in appearance or as elaborate as your budget allows. Display cases don't have to be brand-new. A clean, used unit in good condition works just as well in many cases. You might even want to consider a used department store display case, they come in many shapes and sizes. Department store display cases can be equipped with lights, and usually have adjustable glass shelves. Whatever your particular choice is, be flexible in your thinking and exercise some creativity to house your displayed collectible items.

95

"MU
30th

CHAPTER ELEVEN

MUSTANG MISCELLANEOUS

Among the hundreds of Mustang collectibles reviewed for inclusion in this book, many didn't fall into a category or chapter. Reviewing the contents of this chapter will help you realize how vast the array of Mustang paraphernalia is that has been created over the years. The following items are just some of the more interesting Mustang collectibles.

Paper Ponies

Automotive product pamphlets, aftermarket catalogs, promotional flyers, postcards, or any special printed items made of paper or cardstock have always been very collectible and this is especially true for Mustang ephemera. Over the nearly 40 years of Mustang's continuous production, there have been literally hundreds of pieces of Mustang paper ephemera produced. Of particular interest to collectors are materials dealing with their favorite pony, a specific car, or items that highlight past Mustang exploits or forecast the future of the marque.

This 30th anniversary porcelain plate titled, "1964 Mustang 1994, What was then is now," measures 8-1/2 inches in diameter. Based on artwork by Paul H. Adams, The American Rails and Highways Company produced this item to commemorate the new Generation IV pony in 1994; note the dust-proof Plexiglas display case.

This greeting card features the front end of a first-generation Mustang. It's a die-cut item cut from a single piece of cardstock and hinged in the middle. There is no inscription printed on the inside. However, on the back panel are two paragraphs of Mustang information. This Mustang card was part of a two-package, 12-card set produced by Paper House Productions in 1985. To write on the Mustang greeting card you could use this laser-etched, anodized Mustang ballpoint pen; manufacturer unknown. This pen was purchased recently through the Ford Motorsports catalog.

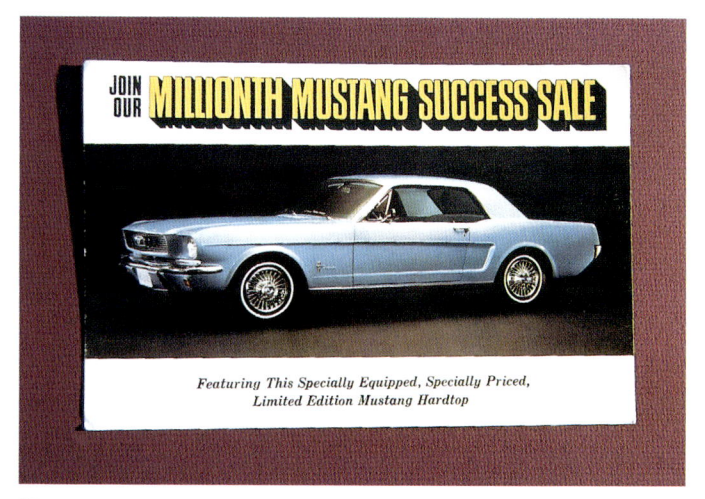

Shown is a commemorative postcard that promoted a special "Millionth Mustang Success Sale," which featured a 1965 Mustang coupe equipped with the standard 200-cid inline six-cylinder Ford engine in what was called the Sprint version of the pony.

Molded Mini-Mustangs

The collectible Mustang miniature cars included here are made from a wide variety of mostly unrelated materials. Although they don't fall into clearly defined categories, each product type has been cast in molds of one type or another. Glass, ceramic, porcelain, resin, and pewter have been used to create some of the lasting Mustang mementos. Although none of these specific Mustang collectibles can be classified as Mustang toys, models, or scale replicas, the origins of their appearance is clearly discernible.

After an absence of nearly a dozen years, Ford Motor Company returned to major-league motorsports with the Miller Mustang that competed in the IMSA Grand Touring series in 1981. The backside of the card contains technical data on the racecar, plus a brief profile of driver Klaus Ludwig. The card was a product of the Miller Brewing Company.

Some of the items shown here are nearly 40 years old. Others are currently available from retail stores and mail-order sources. Obviously, vintage products are more sought after by serious Mustang collectors, and harder to find, compared to newly manufactured products. Things that are readily available and affordable today may well be tomorrow's sought-after Mustang collectibles. Personal tastes, and the size of your pocketbook, will dictate what populates your collection. The standard rule is: If it appeals to you, buy it now! It will probably never be more available or affordable than right this moment.

Mustang Gear

Mustang apparel is probably the most often purchased and popular pony paraphernalia, but possibly the least collected. Clothing is so scarce and least collected because it's worn by the owner until it's faded, frayed, lost, or damaged.

Over the nearly 40 years of Ford Mustang, there have been literally tens of millions of hats, T-shirts, sweatshirts, jacket patches, and jewelry items produced. T-shirts have been emblazoned with countless logos, photographs, and illustrations that depict the sentinel moments in the history of the marque. Subjects range from original illustrations and drag racing action to special-interest Mustangs such as Shelbys and Saleens.

A few clothing items were not worn and have been retired for preservation. Other clothing items survived with little wear and tear against the ravages of time. Many of these items have survived, and newly produced products remain among the most popular today with collectors.

This large four-color postcard commemorates Tommy Kendall's SCCA Trans-Am championship in 1996 when Ford took the series' manufacturers' title. This sample is signed by Kendall, which makes this card very collectible.

Mustangs in Print and on Film

Ford Mustang mania has resulted in a proliferation of paraphernalia as inclusive and widespread as one's imagination. Sales literature, plastic model kits, diecast cars, toys, after-shave bottles, apparel, books, calendars, clocks, porcelain Christmas tree bulbs, whisky decanters, signs, and posters are all sought-after items today by Mustang collectors. It should not surprise us that such a significant American icon as the Mustang would be a popular movie and television prop. So far, there haven't been any possessed ponies, talking 'Stangs, or Mustangs that leap tall obstacles in a single bound. For now, we'll have to leave that sort of thing to the likes of "Christine," "Herbie," or the "General Lee." But, many Mustangs *have* provided transportation and excitement in films and television programs.

Feature Films

A short list of popular feature films with a Mustang(s) playing sidekick to the main character include:

James Bond movies:
- *Goldfinger* (1964) featured a 1964 white convertible.
- *Thunderball* (1965) featured a 1965 blue convertible

This color postcard of the 1994 Mustang SVT Cobra coupe shows a variety of views of the potent pony. On the backside is an extensive listing of technical information and performance features.

The Rebellious Sixties

In 2000, the U.S. Postal Service released a series of 10 stamp sets commemorating events in each of the 10 decades of the twentieth century. Included in the 1960s set was this stamp of a 1964-1/2 Mustang convertible.

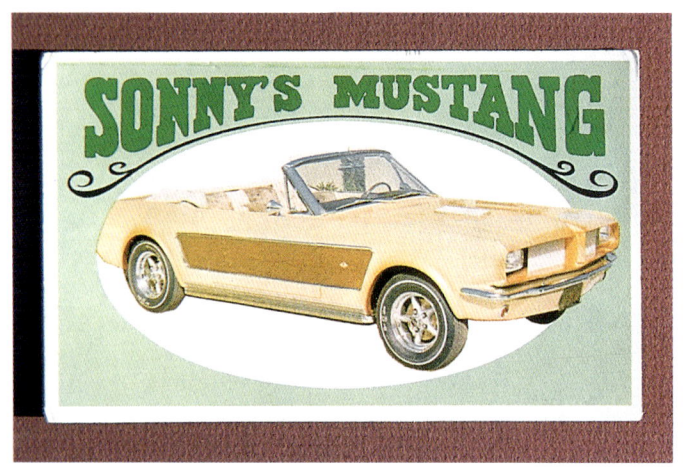

This Sonny and Cher trading card was originally part of a 36-card series released in 1970 under the name "Way Out Wheels."

These three Mustang trading cards are part of a 66-card set titled "Odder Odd Rod Cards." The set was originally issued in 1972 and may still be found at card shops or card collector swap meets.

•*Diamonds Are Forever* (1971) featured a bright red 1971 Mach I careening up and down the streets of Las Vegas.

Other Hollywood films with a Mustang as the primary wheels read like a who's who of movieland:

•*Gone in 60 Seconds* (1974) featured a full-throttled, mustard yellow Mach I on the prowl.

•*Nightmare in Badham County* (1976) had Max Baer Jr. in a 1977 Mustang II.

•*Coming Home* (1978) had Jon Voight and Jane Fonda darting around in a modified 1968 GT500.

•*Starman* (1985) featured Karen Allen and her alien captor, played by Jeff Bridges, in a 1977 Cobra II.

•*Innerspace* (1987) included clips of Meg Ryan and Dennis Quaid in a 1967 convertible.

•*Malone* (1987) starred Burt Reynolds, whose primary ride was a 1969 Mach I.

•*Bull Durham* (1988) featured Kevin Costner and Susan Sarandon cavorting around in a 1968 Shelby and a 1988 GT convertible.

•*Hard to Kill* (1988) featured Steven Seagal in a white 1988 GT convertible.

•*Twins* (1988) had Arnold Schwarzenegger and Danny DeVito tooling around top-down in a new GT convertible.

•*Marked For Death* (1990) put Steven Seagal at the wheel of a sinister black 1973 Mach I which didn't survive in the early scenes of this film.

•*Basic Instinct* (1992) saw Sharon Stone at the wheel of a 1991 GT convertible.

•*The Jerky Boys* (1995) had an absolutely outrageous 1973 Mustang stretch limo.

•*Assassins* (1997) featured Antonio Banderas doing duty in a 1997 GT.

•*The Thomas Crown Affair* (1999) had Pierce Brosnan and Rene Russo in a 1967 Shelby Mustang convertible.

•The *Gone in 60 Seconds* (2000 remake) featured Nicolas Cage taking care of business at the wheel of a modified 1967 GT500.

•And there are many more movies featuring a Mustang including *Fatal Beauty*, *52 Pickup*, and *Sleepwalkers*.

No Fooling...

Although the 1994 movie *Nobody's Fool* didn't feature a Mustang as part of the story line, nor was it even used as general transportation, the movie would become a significant part of the marque's history. Actor Paul Newman played the lead in the movie and received an Academy Award nomination for Best Actor. On his 70th birthday, Newman, who is also an accomplished racecar driver, drove a *Nobody's Fool*–sponsored Mustang to the class championship at the 1995, 24 Hours of Daytona at the Daytona International Speedway.

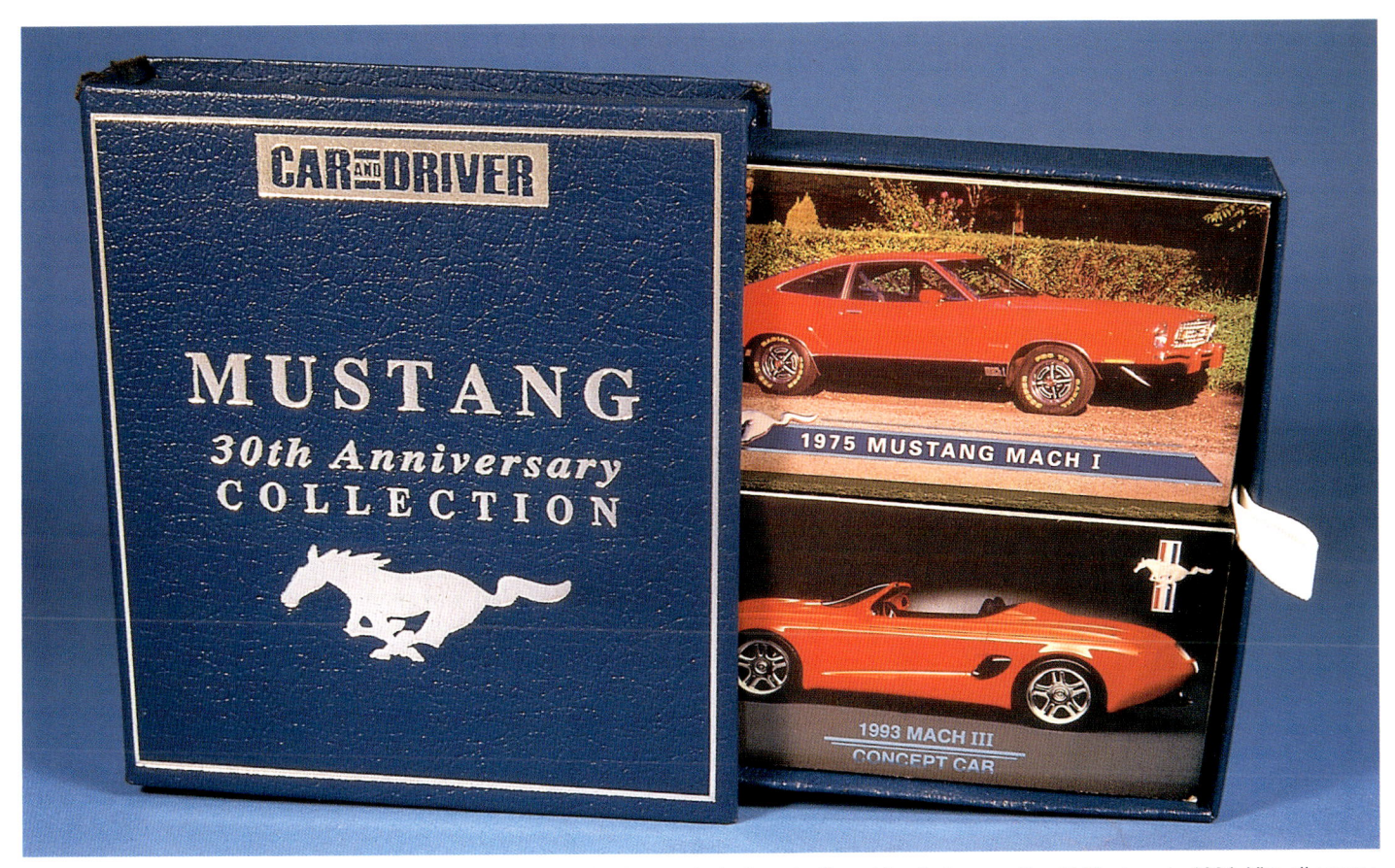

This is a special commemorative trading card set produced by Ford to mark the introduction of the first-generation IV Mustang in 1994. Virtually every model and body style of Mustang from April 1964 to 1994, along with Shelbys and various show cars from different eras, are included in the more than 80-card set.

Many television programs over the years have used Mustangs as a central prop. They include:
- *Charlie's Angels*
- *Spencer For Hire*
- *Jake and the Fat Man*
- *Partners in Crime*
- *Mickey Spillane's Mike Hammer*
- *Reasonable Doubts*
- And the new *Knight Rider* series used a Generation IV Mustang.

This color cardboard 1965 Mustang was used to serve up French fries at many popular fast-food chains. This sample item, No. 2716, was manufactured by the Admark Company in Topeka, Kansas, in 1995.

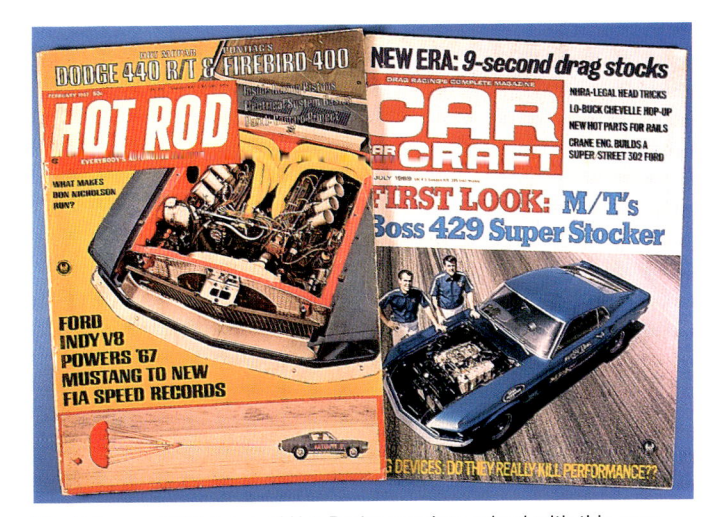

The February 1967 issue of Hot Rod magazine arrived with this spectacular color cover that featured this Indy V-8 that was placed in a 1967 Mustang fastback GT. The article announced Ford's assault on FIA land speed records in the 200 miles per hour region. The July 1969 issue of Car Craft magazine exploded with this dynamic aerial view of Butch Leal, the late Mickey Thompson, and their spectacular Boss 429 NHRA super stocker. This magazine included a multi-page feature titled "War Toy" that took an in-depth look at the Leal/Thompson 'Stang.

101

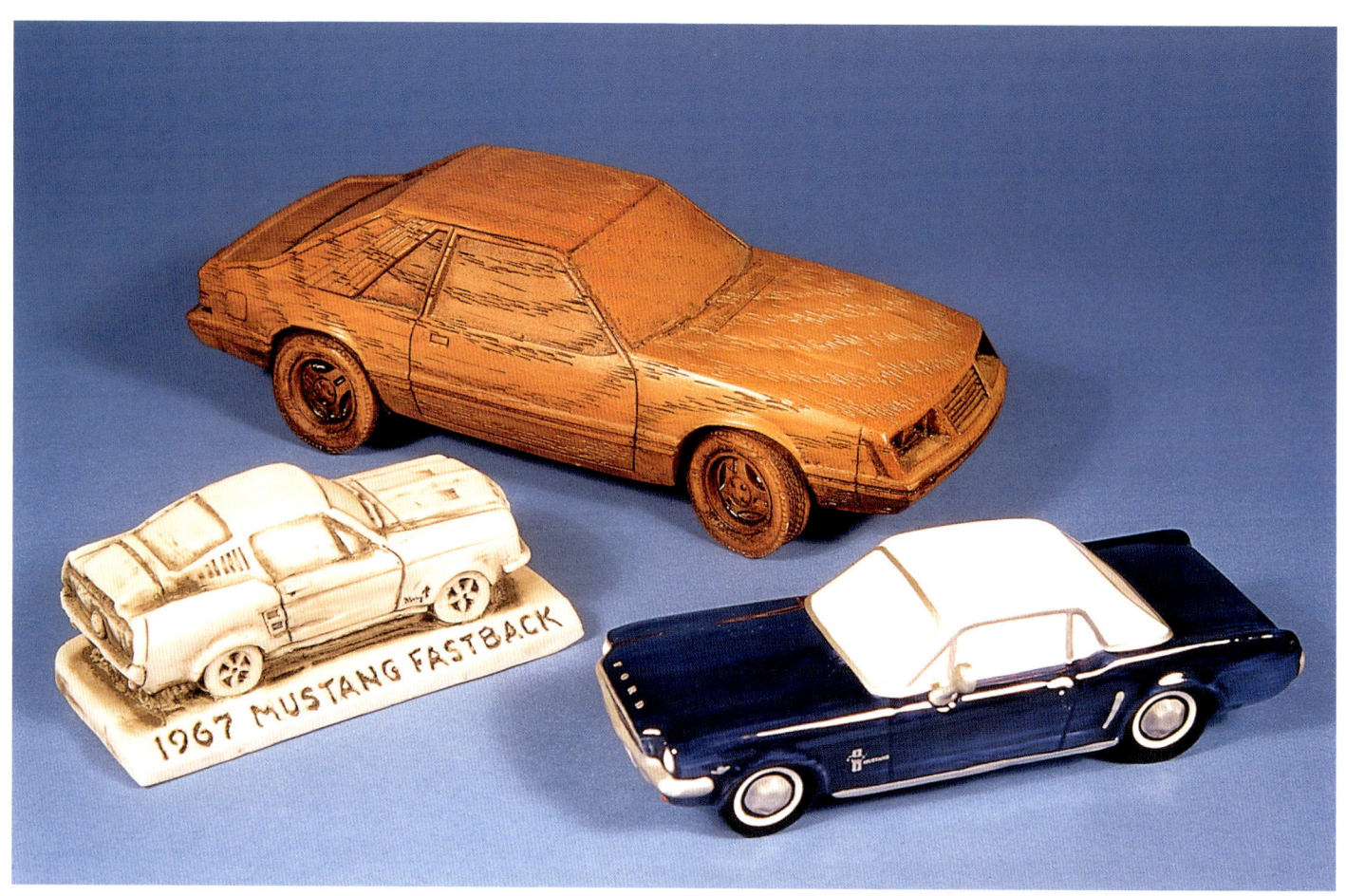

Shown are three Mustangs represented in synthetic marble, cast-resin, and porcelain materials. At left is a Marble Mountain Creations 1967 Mustang caricature sculpture (No. 91 of 10,000 pieces); a 1/24th scale cast-resin 1983 Mustang LX from Daytona Beach Trophies; and a porcelain 1965 Mustang coupe from the Department 56 "The Original Snow Village Collection" line. There's a choice of three such 1965 Mustangs: red, yellow, and blue over white.

The Avon Company has created numerous automotive subjects in their men's after-shave and cologne line. This 1965 Mustang coupe in glass and molded plastic will never pass as a scale replica of the first-generation pony, but it remains a sought-after Mustang collectible. Tai Winds after-shave doesn't smell anything like high-octane fuel either!

This set of Mustang beverage coasters was recently purchased through the Ford Motorsports catalog. The manufacturer is not identified on the product or packaging material.

This Jim Beam porcelain whisky decanter measures out to about 1/14th scale. This item was produced in 1985 and closely resembles the original 1964-1/2 Mustang. The decanter was originally produced in ivory (most common), red, and black (most rare).

Any Mustang enthusiast would feel like they've reached nirvana eating a seven-course gourmet dinner served on this officially licensed dinnerware from The American Rails and Highways Collection by Michael Leson Designs in Youngstown, Ohio.

This is a set of four 12-ounce, lead-free crystal Mustang drinking glasses. From left: the galloping pony, the three-color Mustang logo, the Cobra crest, and the GT Chevron badge. This set was recently ordered through the Ford Motorsports catalog, and the manufacturer is not identified on the items or packaging material.

The four coffee mugs shown here were part of a five-cup set offered through Ford dealer's parts departments in 1989. The set includes the Mustang Probe racecar, 1989 GT convertible, 1971 Mach I, and a 1965 GT convertible. The fifth cup commemorated Bill Elliott's 1988 NASCAR championship. There's no explanation why the five-piece set was comprised of four Mustang mugs and one Thunderbird mug.

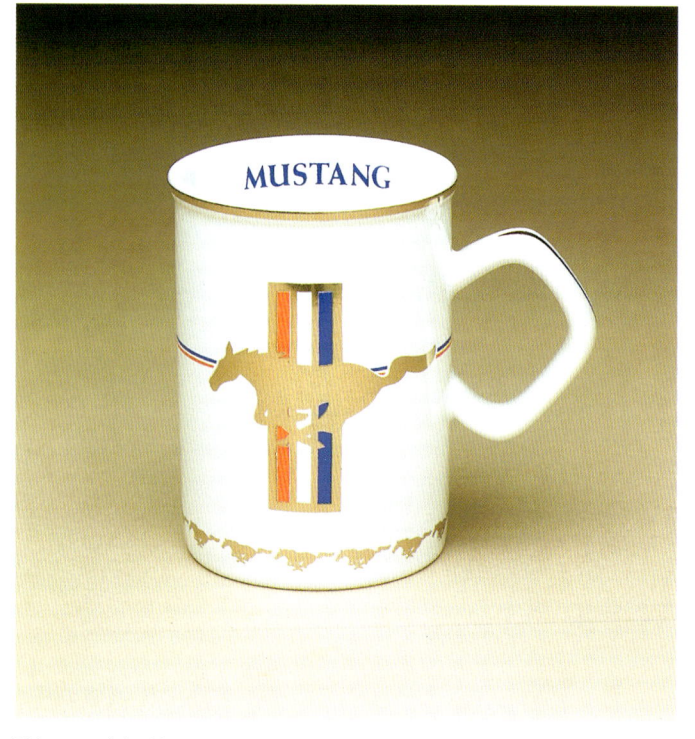

This pewter 1965 Shelby Mustang GT350 desktop plaque was created in 1980 for Shelby Mustang collectors and owners by K.A.R. Enterprises in Floral Park, New York. The original retail price was $19.95, but don't expect to find one today in this good condition with that price!

This porcelain Mustang coffee mug is the product of The American Rails and Highways Collection. Although it was originally designed as part of the Mustang dinnerware set, this item is available for sale separately.

104

For Mustang enthusiasts who consume beer, these two handsome steins are just the ticket for savoring your favorite ale. At left is a Budweiser stein which commemorates the 1964-1/2 'Stang from the Anheuser-Busch Classic Cars series. At right is a stein from PMI, which was obviously done to commemorate the introduction of the Generation IV Mustang with the original red 1965 and yellow 1994 cars depicted. This item was originally available through Ford dealerships.

Shown is a variety of Mustang apparel including two oval jacket patches, a silk tie featuring a selection of colorful illustrations of classic 'Stangs, and an SVT Cobra hat from John Coulter's collection.

This is certainly a rare piece in the United States. Here is a souvenir hat to commemorate the 35th Anniversary Mustang Celebration that was held in Adelaide, Australia, in 2000.

105

This silver coin set was commissioned by Ford in 1999 to commemorate the 35th anniversary of the Mustang. There are coins representing the 1964-1/2, 1970, 1984, 1994, and 1999 Mustangs.

This is certainly an eclectic assortment of Mustang hat pins. Horizontally at the top of the photograph are a variety of prancing ponies and full-tilt Mustang emblems in many styles. At the bottom from the left: a pin given to participants at the 1989 Hot Rod Nationals model car contest in Indianapolis, Indiana; one given to contributors to *Scale Auto Enthusiast* magazine's special Mustang issue, No. 65; a pin commemorating George Follmer at the wheel of a Bud Moore Trans-Am Mustang in 1970; and one commemorating Tommy Kendall's GT title in a Roush Mustang at Daytona in 1993.

This trio of Mustang key fobs represents the variety of quality items that have been available over the last 30-plus years.

Shown is an original issue 1979 Indy 500 Mustang pace car jacket. This is the lined version, and there was also an unlined jacket offered with the same basic design.

This is the first style of jacket patches that were given to members of the original National Mustang Owner's Club. This is from the Paul McLaughlin collection.

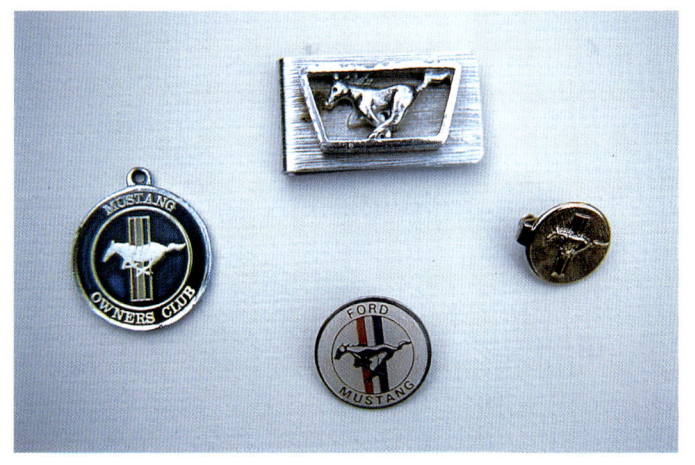

This is one of the very first jacket patches that was part of the membership package that came to new Mustang owners joining the National Mustang Owner's Club.

Shown is an assortment of inexpensive Mustang hat pins produced in the mid-1980s.

107

The Snap-On Tools men's jewelry box was a limited-production item created to commemorate the 30th anniversary of Mustang in 1994. This item may still be available today from selected Snap-On Tools dealers. This one is loaded with many collectible Mustang jewelry pieces.

This 25th Anniversary Mustang hand towel came from New Zealand in 1989. It measures 13-1/2 inches by 17 inches.

Here is a pair of Mustang watches that are currently available. At left is an example purchased from the Danbury Mint. A closer inspection of the paperwork reveals the item is actually the Ford Mustang "American Pride" watch made by Taxor Inc. in Azusa, California. At right is a Europa ILC watch that was ordered through the Ford Motorsports catalog.

108

This car is indisputably the most notable Mustang ever to appear on film. The movie *Bullitt* contains the granddaddy of all great car chase sequences. The chase on the hilly streets of San Francisco is on between Frank Bullitt (played by the late Steve McQueen) in his modified 1968 GT390, and the bad guys in their sinister black 1968 Charger R/T. Some 25 years later, the movie continues to be a bestseller at video stores nationwide. The dark green pony is still very popular, and in 2001, Ford produced a special Bullitt GT Mustang. This is the DVD version of the 1968 film displayed along with the Revell-Monogram 1968 Mustang GT390 1/24th scale diecast model and a hand-painted Frank Bullitt resin figure.

The premise of the 1974 cult-classic film *Gone in 60 Seconds* was to steal 48 cars and not get caught. The lead character was named Mandrian Pace, played by the movie's director H.B. Halicki, who sat behind the wheel of "Eleanor," a souped-up 1971 Mustang Mach I.

The movie was remade in 2000, with Nicholas Cage in the lead role. The central automobile was a modified 1968 Shelby Mustang. Originally, Revell-Monogram was scheduled to produce a diecast model of the new Eleanor, but was unable to obtain licensing rights to the movie vehicle. Instead, Revell-Monogram is planning (at this writing) to manufacture a similar street-stock 1968 Shelby Mustang GT500 in metal. Here is the DVD of the original *Gone in 60 Seconds* movie with an original 1971 Mustang Mach I promotional model molded in Grabber Orange, a mustard or pumpkin color, which just happens to be the color of "Eleanor."

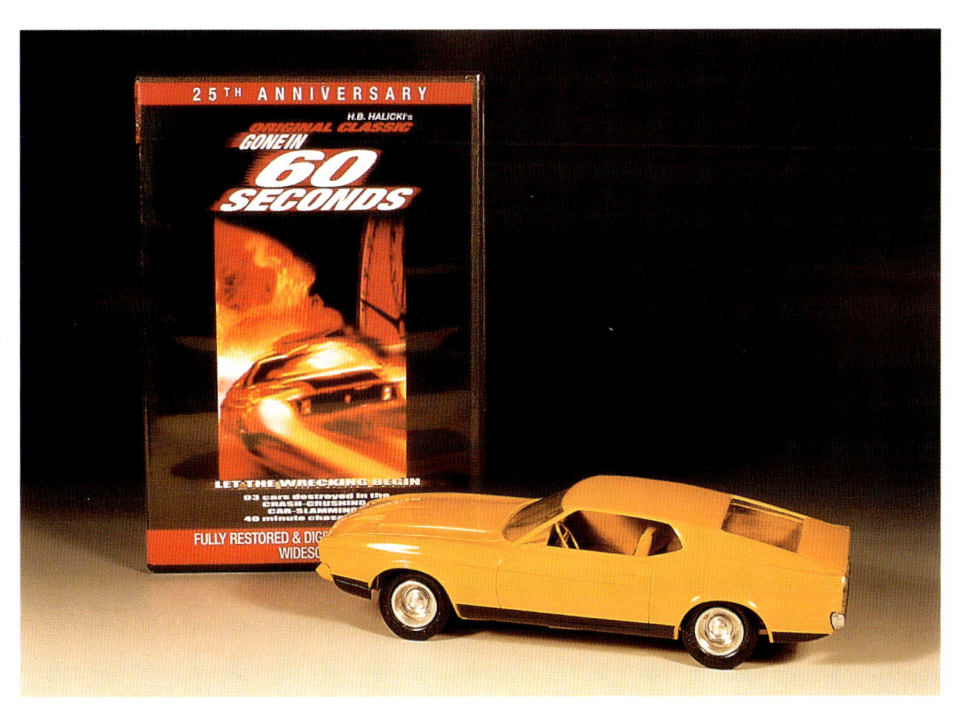

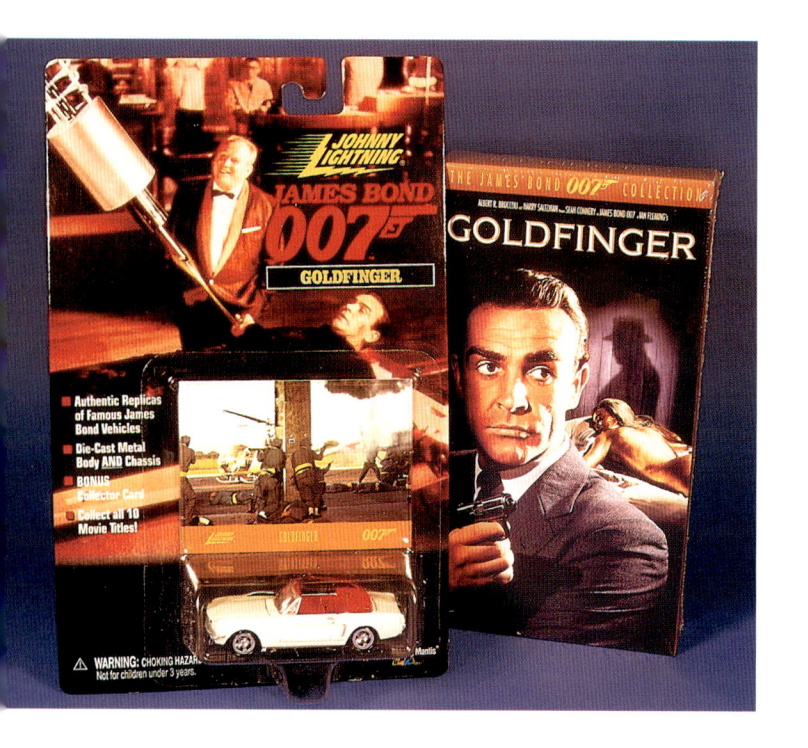

One of the first blockbuster James Bond films was the 1964 release, *Goldfinger*. Sean Connery was cast as the famous secret agent 007 who was "licensed to kill." The plot centered on the Bank of England when it discovered someone was stockpiling vast quantities of gold. The suspected villain was international bullion dealer Auric Goldfinger. James Bond was sent to investigate. As the plot thickens and the location changes to the United States, a courier driving a white 1965 Mustang convertible meets a crushing demise. Shown is the blister pack of the *Goldfinger* 1/64th scale diecast Mustang convertible and the VHS version of the movie.

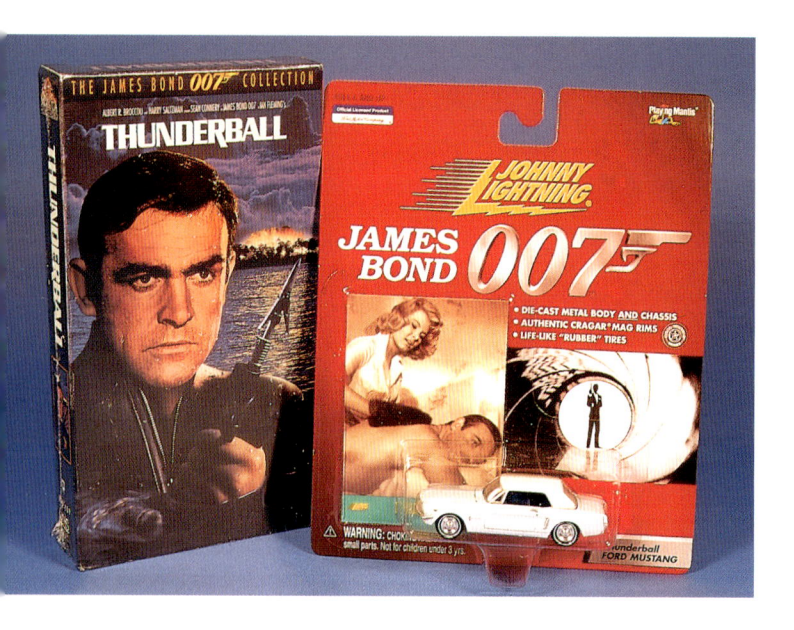

Thunderball was a best-selling book for Ian Fleming, and an equally popular movie in 1965, based on British Secret Service agent James Bond. The movie plot centers on SPECTRE's theft of a British Vulcan bomber containing a pair of atomic bombs. The nefarious band of terrorists holds NATO hostage to the tune of $200,000,000! A fetching young blond in a powder blue Mustang has the misfortune of crossing paths with a "road hog" Bond. Cut to the chase of a typical slice of movieland special effects. Here is the VHS version of *Thunderball,* with the blister pack of the sky blue 1965 Mustang convertible model diecast of the movie car.

One of the last Bond films starring Sean Connery in the lead role was *Diamonds Are Forever,* which was released in 1971. After traveling the globe in an attempt to eliminate arch-rival Blofeld, Bond returns triumphant only to find out that huge amounts of diamonds are being stolen from mines in South Africa, and two assassins methodically bump off all of the smugglers involved. Bond goes undercover to investigate and discovers that the chief ringleader is Blofeld. There's a raucous police chase up and down the well-lit streets of downtown Las Vegas with Connery and Jill St. John in a bright red Mustang Mach I. This pony was the match for any chase car, and proved that resting on one's laurels is not always a bad thing! Shown is a pair of special diecast Mustangs plus the VHS version of the popular James Bond movie *Diamonds Are Forever*. The 1971 Mustang 1/43rd scale model at left is produced by British manufacturer Corgi. This experienced manufacturer is currently offering an expanded series of James Bond movie vehicles. At right is the same 1971 Mustang from the movie in 1/64th scale made by Polar Lights' Johnny Lightning.

On his 70th birthday, Paul Newman drove the *Nobody's Fool*–sponsored Mustang to the class title at the 1995, 24 Hours of Daytona at the Daytona International Speedway. With this accomplishment, Newman is the oldest individual to ever win a major motorsports title, and he did it in a Ford Mustang racecar.

There are a number of excellent DVDs and videos about Mustangs. The History Channel, as part of its automotive series, ran a one-hour program about the development of the Mustang through the beginning of Generation IV.
Shown is a two-tape set titled "The Story of Mustang." The set contains a pair of 30-minute tapes that cover many subjects related to the development of the Mustang line, including a variety of Mustang-related automotive subjects.
Also included are three diecast models that relate to the videotapes, but not as a direct product tie-in. From left: a 1/24th scale Bullitt Mustang by Revell-Monogram; a 1/43rd scale 1967 GT 2+2 by Matchbox; and a 1/64th scale Matchbox car of a 1965 2+2.

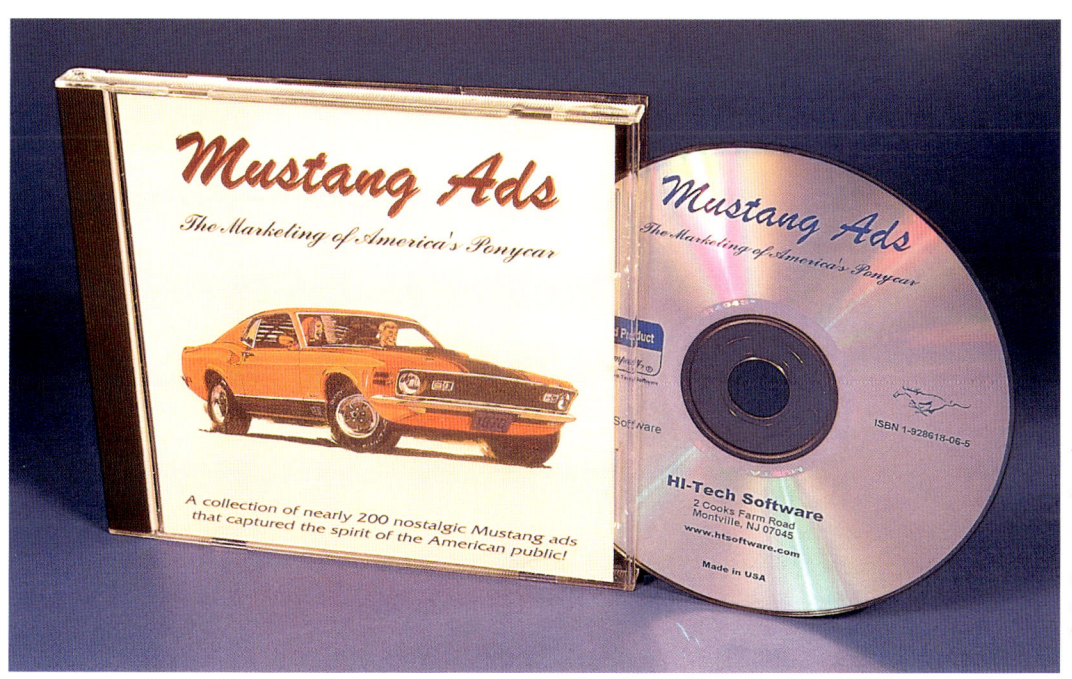

This CD-ROM is titled "Mustang Ads: The Marketing of America's Pony car." The disk is a collection of nearly 200 nostalgic Mustang advertisements that captures the spirit of the American icon. This item was recently purchased through the Ford Motorsports catalog.

111

An attempt was made in the late 1980s to revive the once-popular Monkees television series. Four budding young actors were selected, and scripts were written for the New Monkees. A pilot was shot, and a 1988 Mustang GT convertible with a special marbled light blue paint scheme was prepared for the band's wheels. But the plug was pulled on the series and it never made it to the tube. Shown is Monogram kit No. 2771, which was injection molded with the marbled finish as part of the bare plastic.

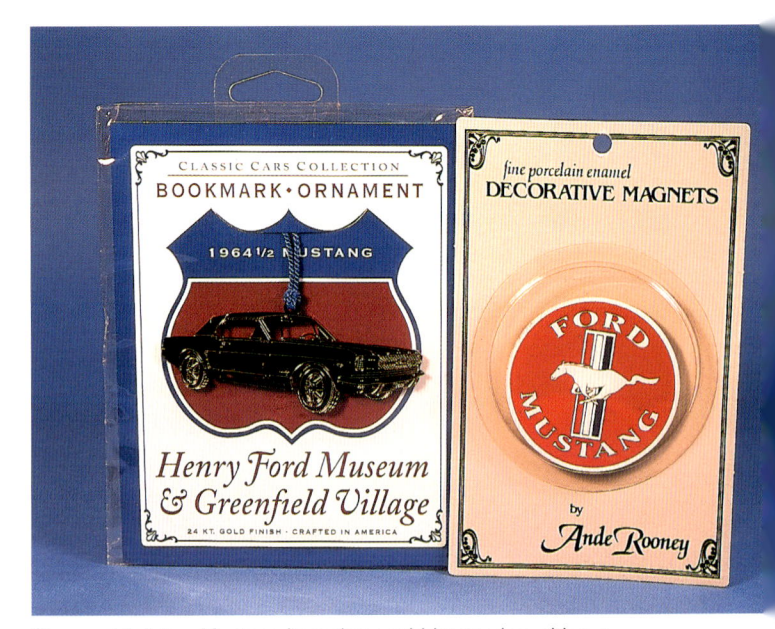

Shown at left is a Mustang item that could be used as either a bookmark or a Christmas tree ornament. Just short of 3-1/2 inches in length, this 24-karat-gold-finished likeness of the original Mustang coupe appears to be photo-etched metal. This piece is produced by Design Master Associates from Williamsburg, Virginia, and bears a 1995 copyright.

At right is a Mustang refrigerator magnet (measuring 2-1/4 inches in diameter) produced by the Ande Rooney company in Highland, New York. According to the text on the back of the packaging material about the manufacturing process, the vibrant colors are finely ground glass crystals that are fired to 1,350 degrees Fahrenheit, which fuses the crystals to a miniature steel backing plate. This is the same process that was used to make early porcelain advertising signs.

The popular Monopoly board game by Parker Brothers Company has been made with many unique themes over the years. This is the Mustang version that was issued in 1999, to emphasize buying, selling, and renting Mustangs to acquire wealth. Among the unique features of this version is how the game's normal venues have been revised to reflect places where you are most likely to find Mustangs such as carports, garages, and dealerships. Even the game pieces have been adapted to the Mustang theme including a 1964-1/2 convertible, a 1965 2+2, and a 1999 coupe!

Shown are three convertible Mustang Christmas tree ornaments. From left is a 1999 Mustang GT convertible by Maisto, originally issued in that year, this sample was ordered from the December 2001 Ford Motorsports catalog; the 1965 Mustang convertible by Enesco was originally issued in the mid-1990s; and the 1966 Mustang convertible was made by the Carlton Cards company and also originally issued in the mid-1990s.

The Department 56 company specializes in unique decorations that include a Christmas line. Shown is their Uptown Motors mid-1960s Ford dealership. Featured along with the structure are three ceramic 1965 Mustangs shown in red, yellow, and blue. Note that the signage on the front picture window of the show room says, "Now on display 1965 Ford Mustang." A closer look inside the building reveals a red Mustang convertible that rotates on a turntable when the lights are turned on.

This string of 1968 Mustang Christmas tree lights is one of the many novel items you may uncover in the search for your pony collectibles. This seasonal item, number UL460, is the product of the Kurt S. Adler Company Inc., from New York.

113

This porcelain Christmas tree ornament was first produced in the mid-1990s as part of The American Rails and Highways series of Mustang collectibles by Michael Leson Designs.

This 1965 Mustang desk clock from Enesco uses a Mustang Christmas tree ornament as the main visual element. This is the same miniature pony used on the Enesco music box.

This is the official John Force phone produced by Columbia Tel-Com in Farmingdale, New York. This is a standard telephone designed to resemble one of Force's late-1990s Mustang Funny Cars. The headlights flash to indicate an incoming call.

This limited-production Fender Stratocaster six-string electric guitar was built to commemorate the 35th anniversary of the Mustang. It features a chromed aluminum body with an engraved Mustang logo, and a Pony badge attached behind the bridge. The famous galloping horse motif is replicated on the ebony fingerboard in mother-of-pearl, brass, copper, and nickel silver. This unique guitar comes with a pale blue carrying bag with a Mustang key fob attached to the zipper. There were only 35 of these manufactured, and none were available for sale to the public. Rumor has it that some executives at Ford have a guitar, as well as the lead guitarist for Kid Rock. The suggested retail price was reportedly $9,000. This special instrument was photographed for the Fender Museum Collection by Pitkin Studio in Rockford, Illinois.

This 1983 Mustang desk pen set was originally produced by the Daytona Beach Trophy Co. According to the accompanying promotional literature, this item was part of a series of popular foreign and domestic sports cars. The base is a faux stone material, and the car is cast from a resin material and is made to appear as though it is carved from wood.

Kay-Bee Toys stores sold this Vanity Fair 1979 Indy 500 radio-controlled pace car in 1979 for $10.

This 1979 Mustang serving tray is a very collectible Ford promotional item. On the backside is a comprehensive history of the car from 1964 to 1979 that highlights all of the special Mustangs. This item was produced in Cleveland, Ohio, by the MTG-79 Company.

This is a rectangular, 30th anniversary Mustang sign (12-3/4 x 16 inches) with illustrations of 1965, 1968, 1984 SVO, and 1994 SVT Cobra Mustangs as the main theme. This sign is produced by the Ande Rooney company in Highland, New York.

This is a 1994-1995 era Snap-On Tools "American Classics" 1964-1/2 Mustang full-color, chrome foil collectible decal.

116

Shown is an unopened can of Wild Mustang Super Premium Malt Liquor that was originally brewed by the Pittsburg Brewery in Pittsburg, Pennsylvania, in the mid-1980s.

This large (13 inches in diameter) analog calendar wall clock (model No. SKU 19291) is available from Taxor, Inc., in Azusa, California. The case is gray plastic with a chrome bezel. The clock sells for less than $50. This Mustang clock was recently seen for sale in the main gift shop in the Henry Ford Museum in Dearborn, Michigan.

117

SOURCES

Fortunately, there seems to be no end on the part of manufacturers to provide collectible Mustang products. For many collectors, the pursuit is as rewarding as ownership. The following list of manufacturers and retailers is a place to start looking for the items shown in this book. I have dealt with all of them and I am a satisfied customer.

Adkins Collectibles, Ltd.
P.O. Box 86
Oak Creek, WI 53154-0086
414-761-1020
www.adkinsstore.com

Ford Motorsports catalog
www.fordcollectibles.com

Model Roundup
443 The North Chase
Atlanta, GA 30328-4252
404-255-1399
www.modelroundup.com
E-mail: roundup@mindspring.com

Motorsports Collectibles, Inc.
Clinton Township, MI 48038
586-263-6513
E-mail: enascar@hotmail.com

Peter E. Hoyt
P.O. Box 15808
Pittsburg, PA 15244
724-378-4840
phoyt@stargate.net

Palmer Motor Racing
8350 Melrose Lane
Los Angeles, CA 90069
213-651-0400
Email: marks930@earthlink.net

Performance Miniatures
615 E. Moss Mill Road
Unit A6
Smithville, NJ 08201
800-931-1227
www.performanceminiatures.com

Taxor Inc.
1201 W. Foothill Boulevard
Azusa, CA 91702
800-282-8332
www.taxor.com

The American Rails and Highways
Michael Leson Designs
7587 Sugarcreek Drive
Youngstown, OH 44512
800-821-3541
www.americanrails.com

Danbury Mint
47 Richards Avenue
Norwalk, CT 06857
800-243-4664
www.danburymint.com
E-mail: customerservice@danburymint.com

Thomas J. Locke & Son
1527 Hanes Mall Boulevard
Winston-Salem, NC 27103
800-574-8483
www.thosjlocke.com
E-mail: office@thosjlocke.com

ThorTek Corp.
2800-A W. Main
League City, TX 77573
800-829-1520
www.thortek.com

PRICE GUIDE

The following statistical material constitutes a value guide for Ford Mustang collectibles. Some of this information was determined based on practical experience, some prices are arbitrary due to the scarcity of particular items, and much is taken from the pages of *The Directory of Model Car Kits* by Bob Shelton and Bill Coulter. Prices for dealer promotional model comes from *Autoquotes, Comprehensive Reference for Annual Dealer Promotionals with Values* by Steve Butler and Clarence Young, and *Promotional Car and Trucks Price Guide* by Steve Butler. Many toy prices are taken from the pages of *Schroeder's Collectible Toys Price Guide*.

Note that the asking price for any of the items listed or shown in this book can vary widely and is dependent on general condition, availability, and current demand. Understandably, there will always be new products coming to market especially for some of the more popular eras. By contrast, original issue items will always be the preferred products due to their dwindling numbers over time. The actual final sale price of any Ford Mustang collectible is the amount of compensation to which both the buyer and seller agree on at the time when product and money change hands.

Page	Item	Price
7	King-K Products, 1/3rd scale cast-resin pedal cars	$100 each
8	1964 AMT 1/25th scale dealer promotional model	$200
8	1996 AMT 1/25th scale dealer promotional model	$35
8	Revell 3-in-1 1/25th scale Mustang kit set #85-6861	$30
9	Matchbox 1/64th scale diecast five-car Mustang set	$25
10	1964 Revell-Monogram Mustang Indy Pace Car kit #2456	$15
10	1979 Revell-Monogram Mustang Indy Pace Car kit #2250	$50
10	1994 Revell-Monogram Mustang Indy Pace Car kit #2975	$15
10	Revell Collection 1/20th scale 1965 GT-350	$175
10	Carrera 1/32nd scale 1965 GT-350 slot car	$50
10	Precision Miniatures 1/43rd scale white metal 1966 GT-350	$200
11	Marble Mountain Creations 1967 Mustang fastback	$15
11	Daytona Beach Trophy Service, cast-resin 1983 LX coupe	$25
11	Avon after-shave glass bottle	$50
12	Johnny Lightning 1/64th scale Mustang diecast	$5
14	Mustang I postcard/folder	$25
15	1964 Ford Mustang press kit	$50
16	IMC 1/25th scale Mustang II kit No. 102	$120
16	Lindberg 1/25th scale Mustang II No. 72169	$10
17	Lindberg 1/25th scale Mustang II built model	$250
20	1964-1/2 dealer sales brochure	$60
20	AMT 1/25th scale 1964-1/2 dealer promotional model	$200
20	AMT 1/25th scale 1964 Indy pace car promotional model	$300
20	AMT 1/25th scale 1965 2+2 dealer promotional model	$225
20	AMT 1/25th scale 1966 coupe dealer promotional model	$175
21	AMT 1/32nd scale 2+2 plastic model kit No.7111	$25
21	Monogram 1/32nd scale 2+2 plastic model kit No. 2000	$8
21	Revell 1/32nd scale (1967?) 2+2 plastic model No. 1250	$10
21	AMT 1/16th scale 1964-1/2 Mustang coupe kit No. 4804	$25
21	AMT 1/25th scale 1964-1/2 coupe plastic kit No. 6154	$200
21	AMT 1/25th scale 1965 "High Roller" plastic kit No. T157	$75
21	AMT 1/25th scale 1965 modified racecar kit No. T180	$180
22	AMT 1965 dirt track Mustang built model kit No. T180	$250
22	AMT 1/25th scale 1966 original annual kit No. 6156	$180
22	AMT 1/25th scale 1966 original 2+2 kit No. 6166	$225

22	AMT 1/25th scale 1966 Cruisin' USA kit No. 2254	$3522
22	AMT 1/25th scale 1966 coupe reissue kit No. 2207	$25
22	Monogram 1/24th scale 1965 GT-350 kit No. 2700	$30
22	Monogram 1/24th scale 1966 GT-350H kit No. 2736	$30
23	Monogram 1/24th scale 1966 GT-350 built model No. 2700	$250
23	Revell-Monogram 1/24th scale 1965 Mustang kit No. 85-4157	$20
24	Revell-Monogram 1/24th scale 1965 2+2 kit No. 2713	$30
24	Revell-Monogram 1/24th scale 1966 GT-350H kit No. 2482	$15
24	AMT 1/25th scale 1966 Sonny and Cher kit No. 907-170	$175
25	Monogram 1/24th scale 1964 Indy pace car kit No. 2456	$15
25	Monogram 1/24th scale 1965 GT-350R racecar kit No. 2969	$20
25	Monogram 1/24th scale 1965 GT-350 kit No. 2700	$30
25	AMT 1/25th scale 1965 slot car kit	$225
26	Aurora HO scale 1965 2+2 slot car	$50
26	F&27F Post Cereals 1966 Mustang toys	$25 each
27	Revell Creative Masters 1/20th scale 1965 GT-350	$200
27	Ertl/AMT 1/12th scale 1964 Indy pace car diecast	$150
27	Revell 1/18th scale 1964 Indy pace car diecast	$100
27	Brooklin 1/43rd scale 1964 Indy pace car diecast	$150
27	Precision Miniatures 1/43rd 1964 Indy pace car white metal	$175
27	Johnny Lightning 1/64th scale 1964 Indy pace car diecast	$10
28	Lane Automotive 1/18th scale 1966 Shelby Mustang GT-350 diecast	$80
28	Lane Automotive 1/18th scale 1966 Shelby Mustang GT-350R	$100
28	Revell 1/18th scale 1964-1/2 diecast convertible	$50
28	Speedy Power 1/32nd scale diecast convertible	$5
28	Matchbox 1965 convertible (TC&V) commemorative	$25
28	Johnny Lightning 1/64th scale diecast convertible	$5
29	AMF original Mustang pedal car	$700
29	Ertl 1/12th scale 1964-1/2 convertible diecast	$100
29	Precision 100 1/18th scale 1964 convertible diecast	$70
29	The Franklin Mint 1/24th scale 1964 convertible diecast	$135
29	Brooklin 1/43rd scale 1964-1/2 convertible diecast	$75
29	Johnny Lightning 1/64th scale 1964 Indy 500 Pace Car	$10
30	Ertl 1/18th scale Tasca Ford Mustang	$80
30	Revell Bullitt 1968 Mustang	$25
30	Brooklin 1/43rd scale 1968 Mustang GT	$75
30	Johnny Lightning 1/64th scale Mustang GT 2+2	$3
32	AMT 1/25th scale 1967 Mustang 2+2 original promotional	$365
32	AMT 1/25th scale 1967 Mustang 2+2 AM radio	$240
32	AMT 1967 Mustang 2+2 kit No. 6631 (new tooling)	$10
32	AMT original 1967 Mustang 2+2 kit No. 6167	$135
33	AMT 1967 Shelby Mustang GT-350 kit No. 6633	$10
33	AMT 1968 Shelby Mustang GT-500 kit No. T397	$30
33	AMT Shelby Drag Team 3-in-1 kit No. T501	$200
33	Nichimo 1/16th scale 1968 Shelby Mustang kit No. MC1601-3500	$75
34	AMT 1968 Shelby Mustang GT-500 kit No. T296	$100
34	Vinyl-on-cardstock 33-1/3 record from kit No. T296	$5
35	AMT 1968 Shelby Mustang built model	$250
35	AMT Autolite Special Hi-Performance Mustang kit No. T-147	$75
35	AMT 1967 Mach 1 prototype show car	$100
36	AMT 1/43rd scale custom 1968 Mustang kit No. M793	$25
36	MPC 1/25th scale Malco Gasser Mustang kit No. 0704	$120
36	MPC 1/25th scale 1968 Mustang 2+2 kit No. 1368	$165
36	AMT 1/25th scale 1968 Shelby Mustang GT-500 kit No. T-296	$100
36	AMT 1/25th scale 1968 Shelby Mustang GT-500 kit No. T-397	$30

36	AMT 1968 Shelby Mustang GT-500 kit No. 6541	$12
36	AMT 1/43rd scale 1968 Shelby Mustang kit No. 3577	$12
37	AMT 1/25th scale 1968 Mustang 2+2 kit No. 6168	$150
37	AMT 1/25th scale custom 1968 Mustang built model	$250
37	Mattel Hot Wheels 1/64th scale 1968 Mustang	$200
37	Revell 1/25th scale 1968 Bullitt Mustang GT	$20
37	Matchbox 1/43rd scale 1967 Mustang	$30
38	Mattel 1/24th scale Hot Wheels 1967 Shelby Mustang	$75
38	Mattel 1/64th scale Hot Wheels 1967 Shelby Mustang	$25
38	Ertl 1/43th scale 1967 Shelby Mustang	$12
38	Ertl 1/18th scale American Muscle 1967 Shelby Mustang	$35
39	Brooklin 1/43rd scale 1968 Shelby Mustang (green, signed)	$1,200
39	Brooklin 1/43rd scale 1968 Shelby Mustang (blue)	$150
40	Monogram 1/24th scale 1970 Boss 302 Mustang built kit	$250
42	AMT 1969 Mustang fastback promotional	$1,000
42	MPC 1/25th scale 1969 Mustang Mr. Gasket Gasser kit No. 725	$130
42	Revell 1/24th scale 1969 Shelby Mustang GT-500 kit No. 7121	$25
42	MPC 1/25th scale 1969 A&W Mustang kit No. 1-2753	$130
42	Revell 1/25th scale 1969 Mach 1 Mustang kit No. 7121	$25
42	AMT 1/25th scale 1969 Mach 1 Mustang kit No. Y905	$50
42	MPC 1/25th scale 1969 Mach 1 Mustang kit No. 1-0731	$50
43	AMT 1/25th scale 1969 Russ Davis Mustang kit No. T-307	$210
43	Monogram 1/24th scale 1970 Boss 429 Mustang kit No. 2282	$35
43	Monogram 1/24th scale 1970 Boss 302 Mustang kit No. 2923	$20
43	Revell 1/25th scale 1970 Mustang Grande kit No. H-1212	$175
43	Monogram 1/32nd scale 1970 Mustang Mach 1 kit No. 1030	$12
44	Polar Lights 1/25th scale Gas Ronda 1970 Mustang kit No. 6056	$15
44	Polar Lights 1/25th scale Blue Max 1970 Mustang kit No. 6507	$15
44	Monogram 1/24th scale 1970 Boss 429 Mustang kit No. 2728	$15
44	Monogram 1/24th scale 1970 Boss 429 Mustang kit No. 2282	$12
45	MPC 1/25th scale 1969 Mr. Gasket Gasser Mustang built model	$250
45	Mebetoys 1/43rd scale 1969 Boss 302 Mustang	$100
45	Ertl 1/64th scale 1969 Mach 1 Mustang American Muscle	$12
45	Ertl 1/64th scale 1969 Mach 1 Mustang Ertl Collection Series	$10
46	Mattel Hot Wheels 1/64th scale 1970 Boss Mustang 30th Anniversary	$25
46	Ertl 1/18th scale 1969 scale Mach 1 Mustang American Muscle	$35
46	Road Champs 1/32nd scale 1969 Mustang Sheriff's Cruiser	$12
46	Ertl 1/64th scale 1969 Mustang Mach 1 American Muscle	$10
46	Revell-Monogram 1/87th scale Mini Exacts 1969 Mustang	$8
47	Ertl 1/18th scale 1970 Mustang Boss 302 American Muscle	$35
47	Matchbox 1/43rd scale 1970 Boss 429 Mustang	$30
47	Mattel Hot Wheels 1/64th scale Boss Mustang	$3
47	Ertl 1/18th scale 1969–1970 Shelby Mustang convertible	$30
48	AMT 1/25th scale 1973 SCCA Trans-Am kit No. T-206	$80
48	MPC 1/25th scale 1972 Mustang Mach 1 kit No. 7213	$130
48	AMT 1/25th scale 1973 Mustang Street Machine kit No. PK-4167	$50
50	Revell 1/25th scale 1973 Blue Max Mustang kit No. 85-7661	$12
50	AMT 1/25th scale 1971 Mustang Mach 1 kit No. T-114	$110
50	AMT 1/25th scale 1972 Mustang Mach 1 kit No. T-335	$125
50	JoHan 1/25th scale 1973 Mustang Funny Car kit No. GC-2100	$25
50	Revell 1/25th scale 1973 Blue Max Mustang F/C kit No. 85-7661	$12
51	Corgi 1/43rd scale *Diamonds Are Forever* Mustang	$15
51	Corgi 1/43rd scale 1972 Mustang Mach 1	$15
51	Johnny Lightning 1/43rd 1972 Mustang Mach 1	$3
51	Ertl 1/64th 1973 Mustang Mach 1	$2

#	Item	Price
51	Johnny Lightning 1/64th 1973 Mustang Mach 1	$3
52	Taiyo tinplate 1973 Mustang Mach 1	$75
52	Matchbox "Gulper" Mustang Funny Car, Speed Kings	$55
53	AMT 1/25th scale 1971 Mustang Mach 1 promotional	$260
53	AMT 1/25th scale 1971 Mustang Mach 1 promotional	$250
54	WEM 1/43rd scale 1974 Mustang II	$25
54	Johnny Lightning 1/64th scale 1977 Mustang Cobra II	$4
56	MPC 1/25th scale 1974 Mustang II promotional	$42
56	MPC 1/25th scale 1975 Mustang II promotional	$40
57	MPC 1/25th scale 1974 Mustang II annual kit No. 7413	$65
57	MPC 1/25th scale 1976 Mustang II Cobra kit No. 1-0773	$80
57	MPC 1/25th scale 1974 Fire Fighter Mustang II kit No. 1761	$75
57	MPC 1/25th scale 1974 Dyno Don Mustang II kit No.1764	$85
58	AMT 1/25th scale 1977 Mustang II kit No. 6560	$35
58	AMT 1/25th scale 1977 Mustang II kit No. PK-4179	$55
58	Gunze-Sanyo 1/24th scale 1976 Mustang Cobra II kit No. G-139-600	$35
58	US Airfix 1/24th scale 1976 Mustang Cobra II kit No. 8133	$30
59	Johnny Lightning 1/64th scale 1977 Mustang II	$3
59	Johnny Lightning 1/64th scale IMSA Mustang Cobra II	$5
59	Jet de Gillette 1/64th scale 1976 Mustang II	$15
60	Revell 1/24th scale 1986 Motorcraft Mustang built kit	$250
62	1979 Indy Pace Car brochure/booklet	$40
62	FW Company 1979 Indy Pace Car go-cart	$1,200
63	UMI 1981 1/25th scale Mustang Cobra promotional	$30
63	MPC 1/25th scale 1979 Mustang Cobra Indy PC kit No. 1-0785	$50
64	MPC 1/25th scale 1979 Mustang Cobra kit No. 1-0725	$55
64	Monogram 1/24th scale 1979 Mustang Cobra kit No. 2260	$35
64	Revell 1/25th scale 1979 Mustang Cobra Turbo kit No. 7200	$50
64	Revell 1/25th scale Mustang Motorcraft Turbo (no kit number)	$60
65	Monogram 1/24th scale 1983 Mustang LX convertible kit No. 2222	$20
65	MPC 1/25th scale "Wild Breed" 1982 Mustang GT kit No. 1-0816	$35
65	MPC 1/25th scale 1983 Mustang GT kit No. 1-0837	$40
65	Monogram 1983 Mustang LX convertible built kit	$250
66	Monogram IMSA Miller Mustang kit No. 2296	$40
66	Monogram IMSA Miller Mustang built model	$250
66	MPC 1/25th scale 1984 Mustang GT kit No. 1-0877	$45
66	MPC 1/25th scale 1984 Mustang 20th Anniversary GT-350 kit No. 0768	$60
67	Monogram 1/24th scale 1984 Billy Meyer 7/11 Mustang kit No. 2710	$30
67	Monogram 1/24th scale 1985 Mustang SVO kit No. 2243	$40
67	Monogram 1/24th scale 1985 Mustang SVO built model	$250
67	Revell 1/24th scale 1986 Folgers IMSA Mustang kit No. 7154	$20
67	Revell 1/24th scale 1986 7/11 IMSA Mustang kit No. 7153	$25
67	Revell 1/24th scale 1986 Motorcraft Mustang kit No. 7155	$27
68	Monogram 1/24th scale 1986 7/11 Mustang IMSA GTP kit No. 2709	$40
68	Monogram 1/24th scale 1986 Motorsports Mustang kit No. 2708	$25
68	Burago 1/24th scale 1983 Mustang Highway Patrol car	$30
68	GMP 1/18th scale 1984 Mustang SVO	$100
69	GMP 1/18th scale 1985 Mustang GT	$90
69	Monogram 1/24th scale 1986 Mustang IMSA GTP built kit	$250
70	Revell 1991 Roush Racing Trans-Am Mustang built kit	$250
72	AMT 1/25th scale 1988 Mustang GT kit No. 30272	$15
72	MPC 1/25th scale 1988 Mustang GT kit No. 6211	$35
73	Revell 1991 Roush Racing Trans-Am Mustang kit No. 7195	$25
73	Revell 1991 Whistler Trans-Am Mustang kit No. 7197	$30
73	Revell 1991 JPS Trans-Am Mustang kit No. 7196	$22

73	Revell-Monogram 1993 SVT Mustang Cobra kit No. 2530	$15
73	Revell-Monogram 1993 SVT Mustang Cobra built model	$250
74	Pro-line 1993 IMSA Roush Racing Mustang built model	$250
74	Minichamps 1/43rd scale 1993 DTM Mustang	$65
75	GMP 1/18th scale Georgia HWP 1986 Mustang LX	$90
76	GMP 1/18th scale 1990 Whistler Trans-Am Mustang	$85
76	New-Ray 1/43rd scale 1990 Mustang GT convertible	$10
76	Ertl 1/43rd scale 1989 Mustang GT convertible (modified)	$25
76	Starter 1/43rd scale 1992 Secret Trans-Am Mustang built model	$250
76	Pro-line 1/43rd scale 1992 Gen. Chemicals T/A Mustang built model	$250
77	Jouef 1/18th scale 1993 Mustang III show car	$40
77	Jouef 1/43rd scale 1993 Mustang III show car	$15
77	Motor Max 1/64th scale 1993 Mustang III show car	$3
77	1998 Mustang SVT Cobra dealer sales brochure	$27
78	Hasbro Winner's Circle 1/64th scale 1999 Superman Mustang F/C	$15
78	Hasbro Winner's Circle 1/64th scale 1998 Elvis Mustang F/C	$15
78	Hasbro Winner's Circle 1/64th scale 1997 Driver-of-the-Year Mustang F/C	$15
80	1994 1/25th scale Mustang GT promotional	$25
80	1995 1/25th scale Mustang GT promotional	$22
81	1996 1/25th scale Mustang GT promotional	$20
81	AMT 1/25th scale Snapfast 1996 Mustang GT kit No. 96-8110	$10
81	AMT 1/25th scale 1997 Mustang SVT Cobra kit No. 97-8231	$15
82	Revell 1/25th scale 1997 Stallion Mustang kit No. 2571	$15
82	Revell 1/25th scale Mustang III concept car kit No. 7364	$15
82	Revell 1/25th scale Boss Mustang kit No. 6390	$12
82	Monogram 1/25th scale 1994 Mustang GT kit No. 2967	$20
82	Monogram 1/25th scale 1994 Mustang SVT Indy 500 PC kit No. 2975	$30
83	Tamiya 1/24th scale 1994 Mustang GT convertible kit No. 24141	$30
83	Tamiya 1/24th scale 1994 Mustang SVT Cobra R kit No. 24156-1800	$35
83	Pro-line 1/43rd scale 1995 All Sports Trans-Am Mustang built model	$250
83	Pro-line 1/43rd scale 1996–1997 All Sports Trans-Am Mustang built model	$250
84	Pro-line 1/43rd scale 1995 *Nobody's Fool* Mustang built model	$250
84	Jouef 1/18th scale 1994 SVT Cobra Indy PC convertible	$80
84	Maisto 1/24th scale 1998 Mustang Cobra	$20
84	Maisto 1/24th scale 1998 Mustang GT	$20
84	New-Ray 1/43rd scale 1998 Mustang GT convertible	$12
85	Auto Art 1/18th scale 1998 Saleen S351 Mustang coupe	$60
85	Auto Art 1/18th scale 1998 Saleen S351 Mustang convertible	$60
86	Action Performance 1/24th scale 1997 Driver-of-the-Year Mustang F/C	$75
86	Action Performance 1/24th scale 1997 Force/Castrol Mustang F/C	$60
87	Action Performance 1/24th scale 1998 Force/Elvis Mustang F/C	$75
87	Action Performance 1/24th scale 1998 Gold/7X Mustang F/C	$75
90	Revell-Monogram 1/24th scale 1999 Mustang Cobra SVT kit No. 85-2525	$15
90	Revell-Monogram 1/24th scale 1999 Mustang "Complete" kit No. 85-2151	$12
90	Johnny Lightning 1/64th scale 1999 Mustang GT convertible	$3
90	Matchbox 1/64th scale 1999 Mustang coupe	$3
90	Mattel Hot Wheels 1/64th scale 1999 Mustang coupe	$3
91	Johnny Lightning 1/64th scale 1999 Pref. Line Prod. T/A Mustang	$10
91	Johnny Lightning 1/64th scale 1999 Homelink T/A Mustang	$10
92	Johnny Lightning 1/64th scale 1999 Mustang convertible	$5
92	Maisto 1/43rd scale 1999 Mustang convertible	$8
92	Maisto 1/24th scale 1999 Mustang GT convertible	$12
92	Maisto 1/24th scale 2000 Mustang SVT Cobra coupe	$10
92	Maisto 1/24th scale 1999 Mustang GT convertible	$12
93	Maisto 1/18th 1999 Mustang GT 35th Anniversary	$25

93	Action Performance 1/24th Superman Mustang F/C	$85
93	Action Performance 1/24th 9X Champion Mustang F/C	$80
94	Action Performance 1/24th Monsters Mustang F/C	$85
94	Action Performance 1/24th 10X Champion Mustang F/C	$75
97	The American Rails and Highways 30th Anniv. Mustang 1964–1994 plate	$45
98	Paper House Productions 1965 Mustang greeting card	$3
98	Millionth Mustang Success Sale 1965 Mustang postcard	$7
98	Miller Mustang IMSA GT postcard	$10
99	Tom Kendall SCCA T/A 1996 Champion postcard, autographed	$15
99	1994 Mustang SVT Cobra performance features post card	$5
100	2000 U.S. Postal Service 20th Century commemorative stamp set, 1960s	$10
100	Way Out Wheels card set, Sonny and Cher trading card	$8
100	Odder Odd Rods card set, Mustangs	$4/card
101	30th Anniversary Mustang 80 trading card set	$35
101	Admark Company 1965 Mustang convertible French-fry box	$7
101	February 1967 *Hot Rod* magazine	$7
101	July 1969 *Car Craft* magazine	$6
102	Marble Mountain Creations synthetic marble 1967 Mustang	$10
102	Daytona Beach Trophies 1/24th scale resin 1983 Mustang	$9
102	Department 56 Original Snow Village Collection 1965 Mustang	$10
102	Avon Company 1965 Mustang Men's after-shave glass bottle	$15
102	Mustang moisture-absorbing beverage coasters, set of four	$16
103	Jim Beam 1964-1/2 Mustang whiskey decanter	$75
103	The American Rails and Highways/Michael Leson Designs Mustang dinnerware	$65
103	12-oz. lead-free Mustang crystal drinking glasses, set of four	$20
104	Ford Mustang porcelain coffee mugs, set of four	$25
104	The American Rails and Highways Collection Mustang coffee mug	$12
104	K.A.R. Enterprises 1965 Shelby Mustang pewter plaque	$55
105	Budweiser 1964-1/2 Mustang stein, Anheuser-Busch CC Series	$35
105	PMI Generation IV Mustang stein	$27
105	Mustang cloth logo jacket patches, current	$3/each
105	Mustang silk tie	$12
105	Mustang Cobra SVT ball cap	$22
105	35th Anniversary Mustang Celebration, Adelaide, Australia, 2000 cap	$30
106	1999 35th Anniversary commemorative coin set, five pieces	$150
106	1989 *Hot Rod* Nationals model contest hat pin	$10
106	*Scale Auto Enthusiast* Mustang issue No. 65 hat pin	$15
106	George Follmer 1970 Trans-Am Mustang hat pin	$8
106	Tommy Kendall 1993 IMSA GT Championship Mustang hat pin	$10
107	Mustang hat pins assortment	$4–6/each
107	Mustang key rings/fobs assortment	$6/each
107	1979 Mustang Indy 500 Pace Car Jacket, new condition	$100
107	Original 1964-1/2 Mustang Owners Club cloth jacket patch	$12
107	First National Mustang Owner's Club members jacket patch	$10
108	Snap-On Tools 30th Anniversary Mustang Men's Jewelry box	$35
108	25th Anniversary Mustang hand towel, New Zealand 1989	$12
108	Taxor "American Pride" Mustang men's watch from Danbury Mint	$35
108	Europa ILC Mustang men's watch, Ford Motorsports catalogue	$55
109	1968 *Bullitt* movie VHS	$15
109	1968 *Bullitt* movie DVD	$25
109	Revell-Monogram 1/24th *Bullitt* 1967 Mustang with figure	$25
109	1974 *Gone in 60 Seconds* movie VHS	$15
109	2000 *Gone in 60 Seconds* movie DVD	$25
110	1964 *Goldfinger* movie VHS	$10
110	1964 *Goldfinger* movie DVD	$25

110	Johnny Lightning 1/64th scale James Bond 1965 Mustang convertible	$4
110	1965 *Thunderball* movie VHS	$10
110	1965 *Thunderball* movie DVD	$25
110	Johnny Lightning 1/64th scale James Bond 1965 Mustang convertible	$4
110	1971 *Diamonds Are Forever* movie VHS	$10
110	1971 *Diamonds Are Forever* movie DVD	$25
110	Corgi 1/43rd scale James Bond 1971 Mustang	$18
110	Johnny Lightning 1/64th scale James Bond 1971 Mustang	$4
111	1995 *Nobody's Fool* movie VHS	$15
111	1995 *Nobody's Fool* movie DVD	$25
111	History Channel Mustang VHS	$25
111	The Story of Mustang, two VHS tape set	$20
111	1965 Matchbox Mustang 2+2	$45
111	The Marketing of America's Pony Car CD-ROM	$18
112	Mustang Monopoly board game	$30
112	Mustang gold bookmark/ornament	$5
112	Mustang refrigerator magnet	$5
113	Maisto 1999 Mustang convertible Christmas ornament	$10
113	Enesco 1965 Mustang convertible Christmas ornament	$20
113	Carlton Cards 1966 Mustang convertible Christmas ornament	$20
113	Department 56 Uptown Motors 1960s Ford dealership decoration	$100
113	Kurt S. Adler Co. 1968 Mustang Christmas light set	$20
114	The American Rails and Highways Collection Mustang ornament	$15
114	Enesco 1965 Mustang desk clock	$25
114	Columbia Tel-Com John Force Mustang Funny Car telephone	$20
115	Fender 35th anniversary Mustang Stratocaster electric guitar	$10,000
115	Daytona Beach Trophy Co. 1983 Mustang LX desk pen set	$35
115	Kay-Bee Toys 1979 Indy 500 Pace Car R/C toy	$25
116	MTG-79 Co. 1979 Mustang metal serving tray	$20
116	Ande Rooney Inc. 30th anniversary Mustang metal sign	$25
116	Snap-On Tools "American Classics" 1964-1/2 Mustang decal	$5
117	Pittsburgh Brewery Wild Mustang malt liquor, unopened can	$8

Index

Allegro, 14
Aluminum Model Toy (AMT) Corporation, 8, 20–22, 24, 25, 32, 34, 36–39, 42, 43, 45–47, 56–58, 63, 72, 80, 81, 87, 95
AMC AMX, 32, 50
AMC Javelin, 32, 50-51
AMC, 32, 50
American Hot Rod Association (AHRA), 23, 74
AMF, 19, 39
Aurora, 26
Auto Art, 87
Bandi, 39
Blue Diamond Classics Company, 7
Branson, Dick, 23
Brown, Keith, 85
Bud Moore Engineering, 44
Bundy, Doc, 68
Burago, 68
Carrera, 10
Cars and Concepts, 63
Chevrolet Camaro, 32, 42, 50, 56, 64, 73, 91
Cogan, Kevin, 67
Coletti, John, 80
Dabrowski, Ken, 80
Dallenbach, Walter Jr., 68
Donohue. Mark, 11, 24, 44, 51, 83
Edlebrock, Cristi, 28
Ertl, 27, 31, 37, 39, 45, 46, 51, 72, 80-81
F&F Mold and Die Works, 26
Ferrari, Enzo, 7
Follmer, George, 44, 51, 106
Force, John, 9, 79, 83, 86-87, 94
Ford Fairmont, 61
Ford, Henry II, 7, 14, 61

Foyt, A.J., 7
Georgia Marketing and Promotions (GMP), 68, 75
Glidden, Bob, 44, 56, 83
Gloy, Tom, 68
Grove, Tom, 34
Gurney, Dan, 14
Halsmer, Pete, 75
Harper, Peter, 22
Hasbro, 79
Holman-Moody, 23, 24, 35
Iacocca, Lido "Lee", 7, 14, 16, 17, 24, 55, 61
Indianapolis 500, 7, 63, 82
Industro-Motive Corporation (IMC), 16-17
International Hot Rod Association (IHRA), 23
International Motor Sports Association (IMSA), 57
Jack Roush Engineering, 63, 68
Jenner, Bruce, 68
JoHan, 95
Johnson, Bob, 24
Jones, John, 68
Jones, Parnelli, 9, 83
Kar Kraft, 57
Kemp, Charlie, 56-57, 58
Kendall, Tommy, 9, 11, 75, 82, 99, 106
King-K Ltd. Company, 7, 29
Knudsen, Semon, "Bunkie", 41, 55
Lawson, Bill, 23, 24
Lincoln Mark VII, 61
Lindberg, 17, 45
Ludwig, Klaus, 67, 98
Maisto, 87
Marble Mountain Creations, 11
Matchbox cars, 45, 87
Mattel, 37, 38, 45, 87

McLaughlin, Paul, 39
McNamara, Robert, 14
Mercury Cougar, 61, 89
Mercury Zephyr, 61
Minichamps, 87
Model Expo, 47,
Monogram, 41, 43–45, 63–68, 72, 90
Montgomery, George "Ohio", 34, 42, 44
Moore, Bud, 50, 106
MPC, 37, 38, 42, 47, 49, 56, 57, 66, 72
Muldowney, Shirley, 44, 56
Mustang Boss, 9, 41, 43
Mustang Cobra II, 55, 59
Mustang Cobra Jet, 34, 41-43, 64
Mustang GT, 71, 72
Mustang GT350, 24, 38
Mustang GT350R, 24
Mustang GT500, 34
Mustang I, 14
Mustang II, 16, 56
Mustang LX, 71, 72
Mustang Mach I, 8, 9, 41–43, 46, 49, 52, 104
Najjar, John, 7
NASCAR, 23, 44, 67
National Hot Rod Association (NHRA), 23, 74
National Mustang Convention, 90
New York World's Fair, 7, 19, 20
Newman, Paul, 83, 84, 101
NHRA's Factory Experimental (A/FX), 23, 83, 85
Nicholson, "Dyno" Don, 39, 44, 56, 57
Ongias, Danny, 43, 44
Performance Ford Club of America, 59
Pickett, Wilson, 34
Platt, Hubert, 24, 39

Plymouth Barracuda, 32
Polar Lights, 13, 17, 27, 28, 44, 45, 55, 59
Pontiac Firebird, 32, 42, 50, 56, 64, 73, 91
Procter, Peter, 22
Pruett, Scott, 68
Ram Air, 42
Revell, 8, 10, 21, 27, 28, 37, 42–44, 64, 67, 73
Revell-Monogram, 23, 31, 46, 61, 69, 77, 87, 89, 90, 95, 109
Revson, Peter, 44
Ribbs, Wally T., 68
Ritchey, Les, 23
Ronda, Gas, 23, 24, 44
RPM Corporation, 17
Saleen, Steve, 9, 75, 85, 86
Schroeder, Dorsey, 75, 76
Shelby, Carroll, 9, 22, 24, 28, 32–34, 46, 47, 85, 86
Shinoda, Larry, 41
Smith, Ricky, 74
Special Vehicle Operation (SVO), 66, 71
Sports Car Club of America (SCCA), 23
Steeda, 85
Stroppe, Bill, 35
SVT Cobra, 8, 9, 66, 81, 82, 87, 90, 99, 104
Taiyo, 52
Testors, Inc, 17
Thompson, Mickey, 43
Thunderbird, 34, 61, 104
Titus, Jerry, 9, 24, 34, 75
Titus, Rick, 75
Trickle, Dick, 45, 47
Tucker, Stanley, 22
U.S. Auto Club (USAC), 23
U.S. Grand Prix, 14

Other MBI Publishing Company titles of interest:

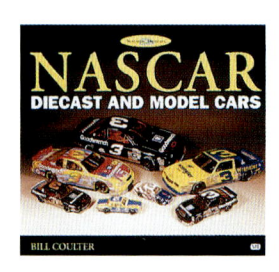

NASCAR Diecast and Model Cars,
ISBN 0-7603-0980-9

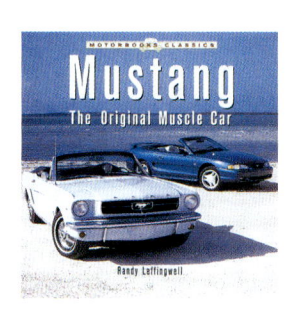

Mustang,
ISBN 0-7603-1349-0

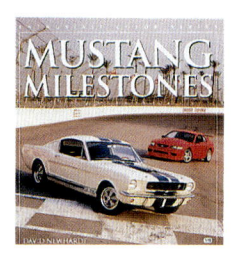

Mustang Milestones,
ISBN 0-7603-0971-X

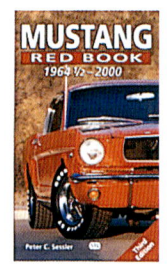

Mustang Red Book 1964–2000
ISBN 0-7603-0800-4

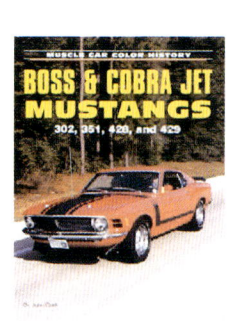

Boss & Cobra Jet Mustangs 302, 351, 428, & 429,
ISBN 0-7603-0050-X

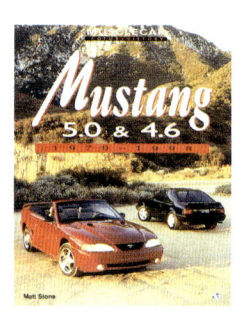

Mustang 5.0 & 4.6 1979–1998,
ISBN 0-7603-0334-7

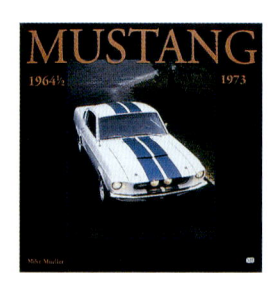

Mustang 1964–1973
ISBN 0-7603-0734-2

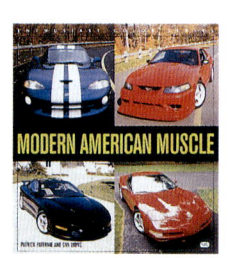

Modern American Muscle,
ISBN 0-7603-0609-5

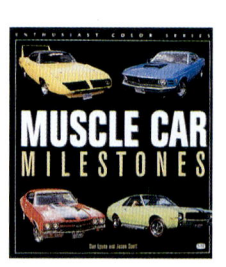

Muscle Car Milestones,
ISBN 0-7603-0615-X

Find us on the internet at www.motorbooks.com 1-800-826-6600